PAST, PRESENT AND FUTURE OF LEGAL ENGLISH

WITH HISTORICAL ANALYSIS, CONTEMPORARY CASE STUDIES AND SPECULATIONS OF FUTURE TRENDS

DR. GOVIND PRASAD GOYAL

Dedicated

to

Guardians of the Rule of Law

Published in 2023

Contents

Contents

Foreword

Legal English is a specialized form of English used in the legal field, and its importance cannot be overstated. In today's globalized world, legal English is essential for effective communication in the legal profession, and it is rapidly evolving in response to changing needs and advances in technology.

The book, "Past, Present, and Future of Legal English," is a valuable contribution to the field of legal language and communication. The book provides a comprehensive overview of the historical roots of legal English, its development, modern legal English in practice, challenges in legal English communication, legal English for non-native speakers, legal English in the digital age, and legal English in the context of globalization.

The expertise of both the authors- Dr. Govind Prasad Goyal and Ms. Archana Singh in legal language and communication is evident throughout the book, and their insights and analysis will be of great value to legal professionals, educators, and anyone interested in the language of the law. Their examination of the future of legal English and its role in promoting ethical conduct and legal education is particularly relevant and insightful.

I highly recommend this book to anyone interested in legal language and communication. It is a well-written and well-researched work that provides a valuable contribution to the field. I am confident that it will become a standard reference for those seeking to understand the past, present, and future of Legal English.

Dr. K.S. Bhati,
Advocate, Supreme Court of India and Former Registrar,
Indian Law Institute, New Delhi.

Preface

English is the lingua franca of the modern world, and its importance cannot be overstated. In the legal field, English has become the dominant language for international communication, and it is essential for legal professionals to be proficient in Legal English.

As academicians and legal language experts, we have taught legal English to law students and legal professionals for many years. We have also conducted research on legal language and communication, focusing on the challenges of legal translation and the impact of technology on legal language.

In this book, "Past, Present, and Future of Legal English," we aim to provide a comprehensive overview of Legal English, its historical roots, its development in the United States, modern legal English in practice, challenges in legal English communication, legal English for non-native speakers, legal English in the digital age, and legal English in the context of globalization.

We also examine the future of legal English, its role in promoting ethical conduct, its importance in legal education, and the emergence of legal English certification programs.

Our hope is that this book will provide valuable insights for legal professionals, educators, and anyone interested in the language of the law. It is our belief that understanding Legal English is essential for effective communication in the legal profession, and we hope that this book will contribute to the development of Legal English as a standardized form of legal language.

We would like to thank our colleagues at IMS Law College in Noida for their support and encouragement throughout the writing of this book and hope that this book will be of value to readers.

Dr. Govind Prasad Goyal

&

Ms Archana Singh

Acknowledgements

We would like to express our sincerest gratitude to all those who have contributed to the creation of this book.

Firstly, we would like to thank the faculty members and students of IMS Law College in Noida for their support and encouragement. We would also like to extend our gratitude to legal language experts, practitioners, and scholars who have generously shared their insights and experiences with us.

We are grateful to the editors and staff at the publishing house for their guidance and assistance in bringing this book to fruition.

We would like to acknowledge the contributions of our research assistants, who have provided invaluable support in conducting research, organizing data, and editing the manuscript.

Finally, we would like to thank our family and friends for their unwavering support and encouragement throughout the writing process.

Thank you all for your support and contributions to this work.

Dr. Govind Prasad Goyal

&

Ms. Archana Singh

Prologue

Legal English is a unique form of language that is essential for effective communication in the legal profession. Its use is pervasive in legal writing, drafting legal agreements, preparing legal opinions, and in various other aspects of the legal field. However, legal English is not simply a form of everyday English, but rather a specialized language with its own terminology, structure, and conventions.

In this book, "Past, Present, and Future of Legal English," we explore the evolution of Legal English from its origins in medieval times to its current use in the globalized world. We examine how Legal English has been shaped by the needs of the legal profession, how it has been standardized in various jurisdictions, and how it has adapted to new technological advances.

The book also explores the challenges of Legal English communication, including the difficulties faced by non-native speakers and the unique challenges of legal translation. We discuss the role of Legal English in promoting ethical conduct and legal education, and we examine the emergence of Legal English certification programs.

The future of Legal English is also a central theme of this book. We explore the potential impact of technological advances, such as artificial intelligence and machine translation, on the future of Legal English. We also consider the role of Legal English in the context of globalization, and the emergence of a global standard for Legal English.

This book is intended for legal professionals, educators, students, and anyone interested in the language of the law. It is a comprehensive and insightful examination of the past, present, and future of Legal English, and we hope that it will provide valuable insights and knowledge for all readers.

About The Authors

Dr. Govind Prasad Goyal, Academician associated with IMS Law College, Noida

Dr. Govind Prasad Goyal is an esteemed author, academician and IQAC-NAAC Coordinator at IMS Law College, Noida. He is a renowned scholar in the field of Legal English and has contributed significantly to the development of the subject.

Dr. Goyal is the author of several books and research papers on Legal English, including the upcoming book on "Past, Present, and Future of Legal English". This book promises to be a comprehensive guide for students, teachers, and practitioners of legal English, exploring the evolution of the language and its contemporary usage in the legal profession.

Dr. Goyal's expertise in Legal English is reflected in his extensive research, which has been published in numerous national and international journals. His contributions to the field have been recognized with several awards and accolades.

As the IQAC-NAAC Coordinator at IMS Law College, Dr. Goyal has played a pivotal role in ensuring the quality of education and academic excellence at the institution. His experience and insights have helped to shape the curriculum of value-added programmes and teaching methodologies at the college, providing students with a comprehensive understanding of legal English and its practical applications.

Overall, Dr. Govind Prasad Goyal's contributions to the field of Legal English are invaluable, and his upcoming book promises to be a significant addition to the literature on the subject. His expertise and insights make him a respected academician and an authority in the field of legal education.

Ms Archana Singh, Academician associated with IMS Law College, Noida

Ms. Archana Singh is a prolific author who holds degrees in both science and law, with a Bachelor of Science (B.Sc.), a Bachelor of Laws (LL.B.), and a Master of Laws (LL.M.) to her credit. She is currently pursuing a Ph.D., and her academic pursuits have led her to author over 10 publications in prestigious journals and books including Scopus and UGC.

Archana's expertise in the field of law is well-reflected in her scholarly contributions, with her works covering a broad range of topics related to the legal framework in India. She has also made significant contributions to books, having authored a chapter in many of them.

Certainly, Archana Singh is not only an accomplished author and academic but also an active member of the legal profession. She is registered as an Advocate and is a member of the prestigious Supreme Court Bar Association (SCBA), which is a testament to her expertise and dedication to the legal field.

ONE

INTRODUCTION

English is one of the most widely spoken languages in the world, and it is used in various contexts, including the legal field. Legal English is a specialized form of English that is used by legal professionals to communicate effectively with clients, colleagues, and judges. However, the use of English in the legal field differs from its use in general everyday communication. Here are a few examples of sentences in both General English and Legal English in the same situations:

Situation: Requesting information from a colleague
General English: "Hey, could you please send me the report by the end of the day?"

Legal English: "Dear colleague, I kindly request that you provide me with the report no later than the close of business today."

Situation: Apologizing for a mistake
General English: "I'm sorry for the inconvenience caused. It won't happen again."

Legal English: "Please accept my sincerest apologies for any inconvenience caused. Rest assured, steps will be taken to ensure that this error does not recur."

Situation: Discussing a deadline extension
General English: "I need some more time to complete the task. Can we extend the deadline?"

Legal English: "I hereby request an extension of the deadline for the completion of the task, due to unforeseen circumstances. I assure you that every effort will be made to finalize it within the new timeframe."

Situation: Confirming a meeting arrangement

General English: "Great! Let's meet at 10 a.m. in the conference room tomorrow."

Legal English: "Thank you for confirming the meeting. I look forward to convening at 10 a.m. tomorrow in the designated conference room as previously agreed upon."

Situation: Discussing payment terms

General English: "Could you please let me know the payment options available?"

Legal English: "Kindly provide clarification on the available payment methods and the terms associated with each option."

From the above exmples, it may be noted that Legal English often employs more formal and precise language, using specific legal terminology and structures to ensure clarity and accuracy in legal contexts.

Legal language is an essential part of modern society, providing a framework for the regulation of our daily lives. From contracts to legislation, legal language is ubiquitous, shaping our interactions with each other and the world around us. However, the language used in legal documents can often be complex and difficult to understand for the layperson.

In this book, we explore the past, present, and future of legal language, tracing its evolution from ancient times to the present day. We examine the impact of historical events, such as the development of writing and the printing press, on the evolution of legal language.

We also delve into the current state of legal language, examining the challenges faced by modern legal professionals in communicating effectively with their clients and the wider public. We explore the use of plain language and the role of technology in simplifying legal language for non-experts.

Finally, we look to the future of legal language and consider the possibilities presented by emerging technologies such as natural language processing and artificial intelligence.

Through a combination of historical analysis, contemporary case studies, and future-focused speculation, this book provides a comprehensive overview of the past, present, and future of legal language. Thus, the book aims to explore the past, present, and future of Legal English and bring forth how has been the journey of legal language in the past, what challenges it confronted in the present and what would be the future trend. Whether you are a legal professional, a student of law, or simply someone interested in the intricacies of language, this book offers a fascinating and insightful exploration of an essential aspect of our society. The book has been designed to have twelve chapters spanning historical aspects, present-day use, and speculations of future trends in Legal English. Other included chapters are as follows:

The Origins of Legal English

This chapter will explore the historical roots of legal English, tracing its evolution from Old English to the Middle English period and beyond. It will examine the influence of Latin and French on legal language, and the role of English common law in shaping legal terminology and concepts. According to Christopher Hutton,

> "*Legal English has a long and complex history that stretches back to the twelfth century and the beginnings of the common law tradition(Hutton 10).*"

Historical analysis of Legal English from Global Perspectives

Legal English has a deep-rooted historical significance and has undergone significant transformations over the course of centuries. This specialized language has had a profound impact on legal systems worldwide, shaping the way law is practiced and communicated. Examining the historical development of Legal English from a global perspective sheds light on its evolution, influence, and current standing in the legal profession.

The Development of Legal English

This chapter will focus on the development of legal English in the United States, including the influence of British legal traditions on American legal language. It will also examine the impact of American legal language on global legal communication and the role of the US legal system in shaping legal English standards. According to Greenbaum and Whitcut,

"*The use of Latin in legal documents began to decline in the late 17th century, as English became the dominant language of the law(25).*"

Modern Legal English in Practice

This chapter will provide an overview of modern legal English, focusing on its use in legal documents, contracts, and court proceedings. It will examine the key features of legal English, including its complex vocabulary, precise syntax, and specialized terminology, and provide examples of how legal professionals use it in their work.

Contemporary case studies on Legal English

Contemporary case studies on Legal English highlight its practical applications and provide insights into the challenges and advancements in this specialized language. By examining these case studies, we can gain a better understanding of the role of Legal English in various legal contexts and its impact on the legal profession.

Challenges in Legal English Communication

This chapter will explore the challenges that legal professionals face when communicating in legal English. It will examine issues such as ambiguity, vagueness, and cultural differences, and provide strategies for overcoming these challenges.

Legal English for Non-Native Speakers

This chapter will focus on legal English for non-native speakers, providing guidance on how to improve legal English skills and navigate the complexities of legal language. It will offer tips on developing legal vocabulary, improving listening and speaking skills, and understanding cultural nuances in legal communication.

Legal English in the Digital Age

This chapter will examine the impact of technology on legal English, including the use of artificial intelligence and machine learning to analyze legal language and support legal professionals in their work. It will also explore the role of digital communication tools in facilitating legal communication across borders and languages.

Legal English and Globalization

This chapter will explore the role of legal English in the context of globalization, examining its role in international business, cross-border disputes, and global legal harmonization efforts. It will examine the challenges of translating legal concepts and terminology across languages and cultures and the potential benefits of a shared legal language.

The Future of Legal English

This chapter will speculate on the future of legal English, examining emerging trends in legal language and communication. It will explore the potential impact of technological innovation, changing legal norms and practices, and global economic and political shifts on the evolution of legal English in the coming decades.

Speculations of Future Trends in Legal English

Speculating on future trends in Legal English involves considering the potential impact of technological advancements, globalization, and evolving legal needs. While the future is uncertain, several possibilities can be envisioned due to rapid transformation in technology and science.

Distinction between General English and Legal English

In this chapter we can see the difference between General English and Legal English in the same situations. For example:

Situation: Expressing an opinion

General English: "I think that movie was really good."

Legal English: "In my view, the evidence presented is highly compelling and supports the judgment that the movie is of exceptional quality."

Legal English and Legal Ethics

This chapter will examine the role of legal English in promoting ethical conduct in the legal profession. It will explore the use of language to express ethical principles and standards, and the role of legal language in shaping ethical norms and expectations.

Legal English in Legal Education

This chapter will examine the role of legal English in legal education, exploring how law schools teach legal English skills and the challenges they face in doing so. It will also explore the importance of legal English proficiency for legal professionals and the benefits of integrating legal English into legal education programs.

Legal English Certification

This chapter will examine the emergence of legal English certification programs, exploring their goals, standards, and impact on legal education and practice. It will also examine the benefits and limitations of certification programs, and the potential for legal English certification to promote greater consistency and professionalism in legal communication.

Common Legal maxims

Legal maxims are concise statements that encapsulate legal principles and concepts. They have been developed over centuries and are widely used in legal practice to guide interpretation and decision-making. We have included a few commonly cited legal maxims along with their meanings, and interpretations.

Conclusion and Future Directions

This final chapter will summarize the key themes and insights from the book, reflecting on the past, present, and future of legal English in legal communication. It will also offer suggestions for future research and innovation in legal English and the potential impact of these developments on the legal profession and society at large.

TWO
THE ORIGIN OF LEGAL ENGLISH

The origin of legal language can be traced back to the development of written language itself. Throughout history, written language has played a crucial role in documenting and regulating legal transactions and disputes. Legal English, in particular, has its roots in the early development of the English legal system, which emerged during the reign of King Henry II in the 12th century (Black 23). However, the influence of legal language extends beyond the borders of England, as it also draws from the Latin language, which was the language of the Roman Empire and remained the language of international law until the 18th century (Global Judiciary 8).

In ancient civilizations like Babylon and Egypt, written language was predominantly employed for legal purposes. It served as a means to record and preserve important legal transactions, laws, and agreements. One of the earliest known legal codes, the Code of Hammurabi, provides us with valuable insights into the development of legal language. This code, written in cuneiform script in Babylon around 1754 BCE, contained a comprehensive set of laws that covered various aspects of Babylonian society, including commerce, property rights, and criminal justice. The Code of Hammurabi demonstrated the necessity of precise and unambiguous language to establish legal norms and ensure fairness in legal proceedings.

Moving forward in history, the development of legal language was greatly influenced by the Latin language. Latin, as the language of the Roman Empire, played a pivotal role in shaping legal concepts and terminology. During the Roman era, legal documents, such as contracts, wills, and judgments, were primarily written in Latin. This widespread use of Latin in legal matters established it as the language of the legal profession and provided a common framework for legal communication across different regions of the Roman Empire.

The influence of Latin on legal language persisted long after the decline of the Roman Empire. As the Roman Empire expanded, so did the use of Latin in legal proceedings throughout Europe. The legal systems of various European countries adopted Latin as the language of their legal practice. This adoption not only facilitated international communication but also ensured the continuity and consistency of legal terminology across different legal systems.

The prominence of Latin as the language of law began to decline in the 18th century with the emergence of national legal systems and the gradual shift towards vernacular languages. As countries developed their own legal frameworks and legal institutions, they started using their native languages for legal purposes. This shift marked a significant departure from the universal use of Latin in legal contexts.

In England, the development of legal language took a distinct path. The English legal system evolved during the reign of King Henry II in the 12th century. As the English courts gained prominence, legal documents and proceedings were increasingly conducted in English rather than Latin. This shift towards English as the language of the legal profession laid the foundation for what would eventually become known as Legal English.

Legal English, influenced by both Latin and the evolving English language, developed its own distinct vocabulary, syntax, and style. It incorporated Latin legal terms that had become entrenched in legal discourse over centuries. Even after Latin ceased to be the dominant language of international law, Legal English retained many Latin expressions and concepts.

The origin of legal language started with the development of written language itself. The use of written language in ancient civilizations like Babylon and Egypt laid the groundwork for the recording and regulation of legal transactions. Latin, as the language of the Roman Empire, then became the language of international law for centuries, shaping legal concepts and terminology. In England, the development of the English legal system during the reign of King Henry II led to the emergence of Legal English, which drew from both Latin and the evolving English language. Today, legal language continues to evolve, reflecting the changing needs and practices of legal systems worldwide.

During its early development, Legal English incorporated various elements of Norman French, resulting in a distinctive French flavor with the adoption of numerous legal terms and phrases from the French language. Notable examples include words like "attorney," "jury," "plaintiff," and "defendant," all of which originated from French. This linguistic influence can be attributed to the Norman Conquest of England in 1066 when the ruling class, which primarily consisted of Norman French speakers, brought their language and legal system to the country.

Over time, however, the English language began to regain its prominence and reestablish itself as the dominant language in England. This shift was fueled by several factors, including the gradual assimilation of the Norman French-speaking ruling elite into English society and the subsequent intermingling of the two languages. The influence of English also grew stronger as the population increasingly embraced and utilized it in various aspects of their lives.

By the late Middle Ages, specifically during the 14th and 15th centuries, Middle English had emerged as the language of the courts in England. This development coincided with a decline in the use of Norman French, as it became less prevalent among the general population. As a result, many French legal terms used in the English legal system at the time underwent a process of Anglicization, where they were modified to align with the evolving English language or replaced with native English equivalents. For example, the term "attorney" was gradually supplanted by the English term "lawyer."

Despite the resurgence of English, certain French legal terms persisted and continue to be commonly employed in the English legal language today. These terms have become deeply ingrained in legal discourse and have retained their original French forms. Examples include "attorney," "deed," and "plaintiff." While their usage has evolved over time and may carry nuanced meanings within the legal context, their French origins are still recognizable.

The enduring presence of French legal terminology can be attributed to a variety of factors. Firstly, legal systems tend to be conservative, holding on to established terminology to ensure consistency and maintain a sense of tradition. Additionally, many legal concepts and principles were initially developed and formalized in Norman French, and their associated terms have consequently become deeply rooted in the legal lexicon. As a result, the continued use of French-derived terms serves to preserve legal continuity and facilitate effective communication within the legal profession.

Legal English initially embraced a distinct Norman French influence, incorporating numerous legal terms and phrases from the French language. However, as English reasserted itself as the dominant language in England, Middle English emerged as the language of the courts, leading to the Anglicization and replacement of many French legal terms. Nonetheless, certain French terms have endured in the English legal language, serving as a reminder of the historical and linguistic interplay between the two cultures.

Here are a few more examples of the origins and derivations of legal terms in English:

Latin Influence:

Legal English is heavily influenced by Latin, especially due to the impact of Roman law on the development of legal systems in Europe. Many legal terms used today have Latin origins. For example:

"In camera" (Latin: "in a chamber") refers to a proceeding or discussion that takes place in private, typically in a judge's chambers.

"Pro bono" (Latin: "for the good") is used to describe legal services provided free of charge, usually for public interest or charitable causes.

French Influence:

The Norman Conquest of England in 1066 introduced French as the language of the English legal system. As a result, many legal terms were adopted from Old French. Examples include:

"Tort" (Old French: "wrong" or "injury") refers to a civil wrong or a breach of duty that results in harm to another person.

"Lien" (Old French: "bond" or "tie") is a legal claim or right over a property as security for a debt or obligation.

Anglo-Saxon and Old English:

Some legal terms have their origins in Anglo-Saxon or Old English, predating the French influence. Examples include:

"Witness" (Old English: "witan" - to know) refers to a person who testifies under oath in court to provide evidence.

"Writ" (Old English: "writan" - to write) historically referred to a formal written order or command issued by a court.

Greek Influence:

Legal English also borrowed certain terms from Greek, particularly in areas of philosophy and democracy. One example is:

"Democracy" (Greek: "demos" - people, "kratos" - power) refers to a system of government where power is vested in the people.

Norman Law French:

After the Norman Conquest, Law French was the official language of the English legal system for several centuries. Many legal terms and phrases were borrowed from Law French, such as:

"Habeas corpus" (Law French: "you shall have the body") is a legal principle that protects against unlawful detention, requiring a person to be brought before a court to determine the lawfulness of their imprisonment.

"Prima facie" (Law French: "at first sight") is used to describe evidence that, on initial appearance, is sufficient to establish a fact or case unless disproven.

These examples highlight the diverse linguistic origins of legal terms in English, reflecting the historical development and influences on the language of law.

The standardization of English as the language of the courts and legal profession was further advanced during the Renaissance period when English common law began to take shape. Legal documents and court rulings were written in a more standardized, formalized style, which led to the development of many legal terms and phrases that are still in use today.

For example, the phrase "habeas corpus" (which means "you shall have the body" in Latin) first appeared in the 14th century and has been a cornerstone of the English legal system ever since. Other key legal concepts that emerged during this period include the presumption of innocence, the right to a fair trial, and the principle of judicial independence.

According to the Indian Judiciary,

> "*The early English legal language was a formidable structure of archaic and scholastic Latin, overlaid with Norman-French legal terms, and garnished with scraps of Anglo-Saxon and Celtic legal usages (Virk, 2004, p. 16).*"

It is believed to have been the product of medieval times when Latin was the dominant language of the legal profession. Latin was the language of the Roman Empire, and its use continued in the legal systems of Europe for centuries. Many legal terms in English, such as "ex parte," "habeas corpus," and "pro bono," are still derived from Latin which remained the language of legal documents and proceedings in Europe until the 16th century. According to legal scholar Bryan A. Garner,

> *"The language of the law has been criticized since ancient times for its archaic style, excessive use of Latin, and abstruse syntax(Garner 29)."*

As the English legal system evolved, the legal language began to incorporate more English terms, although Latin and French terms continued to be used extensively. For example, the English common law system, which was established in the Middle Ages, used terms such as "jury," "writ," and "moot" which were derived from Old English.

One significant milestone in the evolution of legal language can be traced to the adoption of English in the United States' legal system. While legal language in Europe, particularly in England, was heavily influenced by Latin and French, American legal language took on a distinct character influenced by everyday English. This shift is evident in the usage of specific American legal terms that have no direct counterparts in European legal systems. To illustrate this point further, let's explore a few examples.

One notable American legal term is "plea bargain." In the United States, this term refers to a negotiation between the prosecution and the defense, wherein the defendant agrees to plead guilty to a lesser charge in exchange for a reduced sentence or other concessions. The term "plea bargain" succinctly captures the essence of this legal practice, emphasizing the bargaining nature of the negotiation. In contrast, European legal systems may have alternative processes, but the term itself is not commonly used.

Another example is the term "discovery." In American legal language, discovery refers to the pretrial phase where each party exchanges information and evidence relevant to the case. This allows for transparency and ensures that both sides have access to the relevant facts. In European legal systems, similar procedures may exist, but they are often referred to by different names or may not be as comprehensive as the American concept of discovery.

The term "probate" is yet another example of an American legal term that has no direct equivalent in European legal systems. In the United States, probate refers to the legal process of administering the estate of a deceased person, including validating the will, distributing assets, and resolving any disputes. The term "probate" encapsulates the entire process succinctly, while in European legal systems, various terms and procedures may be involved in handling estates.

Bryan A. Garner, a prominent expert in legal language, aptly observes that American legal English is more colloquial, descriptive, and less preoccupied with Latinisms compared to European legal English. This observation underscores the dynamic nature of legal language, which evolves and adapts to the cultural and linguistic context in which it is used. American legal language reflects the pragmatism and accessibility of everyday English, facilitating better understanding and communication among legal professionals and the general public.

Furthermore, the influence of everyday English on the American legal language is not limited to specific terms but extends to the overall style and structure of legal documents. American legal writing often favors clear and concise language, aiming to be comprehensible to a broad audience. In contrast, European legal writing traditionally embraces a more formal and complex style, drawing heavily on Latin and French phrases.

In conclusion, the use of English in the United States legal system marked a significant development in the history of legal language. American legal language, influenced by everyday English, introduced unique terms like "plea bargain," "discovery," and "probate," which have no direct equivalents in European legal systems. The evolution of the American legal language demonstrates its adaptability and responsiveness to the needs of the legal profession and society at large. By employing colloquial and descriptive language, American legal English promotes accessibility and understanding, fostering effective communication within the legal community and beyond.

THREE

HISTORICAL ANALYSIS OF LEGAL ENGLISH FROM GLOBAL PERSPECTIVES

Legal English has a deep-rooted historical significance and has undergone significant transformations over the course of centuries. This specialized language has had a profound impact on legal systems worldwide, shaping the way law is practiced and communicated. Examining the historical development of Legal English from a global perspective sheds light on its evolution, influence, and current standing in the legal profession.

One remarkable aspect of Legal English is its historical foundation in English common law. Dating back to the Middle Ages, Legal English became the language used in English courts and played a pivotal role in the administration of justice. This historical context established English as the language of the law in England and set the stage for its subsequent dissemination.

Colonization and imperial rule further propelled the spread of Legal English across the globe. As English legal systems were introduced to various parts of the world during the colonial era, Legal English became ingrained in the legal frameworks of many nations. The United States, Canada, Australia, India, and numerous African countries inherited English legal traditions, including the use of Legal English. This enduring legacy led to the continued utilization of English as the language of legal discourse, even after gaining independence.

The influence of English common law, with its reliance on Legal English, extended beyond the territories with historical ties to England. Many legal systems worldwide have been influenced by English common law principles, resulting in the integration of Legal English into their legal education and practice. Countries such as Hong Kong, Singapore, Malaysia, and Nigeria, among others, have embraced Legal English due to their historical connections to English common law. In these regions, Legal English coexists alongside local languages, ensuring consistency and clarity in the interpretation and application of legal principles.

The rise of globalization and the internationalization of law has further underscored the significance of Legal English. In today's interconnected world, legal professionals encounter cross-border transactions, international disputes, and the need for harmonization of laws. Legal English serves as a lingua franca for legal practitioners from diverse backgrounds to effectively communicate and collaborate. It enables lawyers to engage in international negotiations, draft international agreements, and participate in international arbitration.

Examples of the global reach of Legal English can be found in international commercial transactions. Agreements, contracts, and legal documents used in cross-border trade are often drafted in Legal English to ensure clarity, consistency, and enforceability across different legal systems. This reliance on Legal English facilitates efficient communication and minimizes misunderstandings or disputes between parties from different jurisdictions.

Research in the field of Legal English highlights ongoing developments and efforts to standardize this specialized language. Scholars and practitioners recognize the importance of clear and accessible legal language to ensure fairness and comprehension in legal proceedings. There have been endeavors to simplify legal terminology, streamline legal writing, and promote plain language principles. These initiatives aim to enhance accessibility and eliminate unnecessary complexity, enabling the general public to understand their rights, obligations, and the legal system.

Proficiency in Legal English has become an increasingly valuable skill for legal professionals in the global job market. Law schools and legal training programs incorporate Legal English courses to equip aspiring lawyers with the necessary language skills for successful careers. International law firms and organizations seek professionals with strong Legal English abilities, recognizing the importance of effective communication in international collaborations and navigating the intricacies of global legal practice.

Thus, a historical analysis of Legal English from global perspectives reveals its deep-rooted significance in legal systems worldwide. Its evolution, from its foundation in English common law to its dissemination through colonization, has shaped the language of the law across diverse jurisdictions. Legal English plays a vital role in international legal transactions and fosters communication and collaboration among legal professionals globally. Ongoing research and initiatives emphasize the need for clear and accessible legal language, as proficiency in Legal English becomes increasingly valuable in the modern legal

One significant influence on Legal English is the historical context of law in different regions. In England, the birthplace of common law, Legal English has a long-standing tradition dating back to the Middle Ages. The language of the law in England was English, and it has been the language used in the courts for centuries. This historical foundation has had a lasting impact on the development of Legal English and its subsequent spread to other parts of the world.

During the colonial era, English legal systems were introduced in various parts of the world through colonization and imperial rule. Countries such as the United States, Canada, Australia, India, and many African nations inherited English legal traditions, including the use of Legal English. As a result, English became the language of legal discourse in these regions, even after gaining independence. This colonial legacy contributed to the widespread adoption of Legal English beyond the borders of England.

The influence of English common law, with its reliance on Legal English, has extended far beyond the English-speaking world. Many legal systems around the globe have been influenced by English common law principles, and Legal English has become an essential component of legal education and practice in these jurisdictions. Countries such as Hong Kong, Singapore, Malaysia, and Nigeria, among others, have embraced Legal English as a result of their historical ties to English common law. In these regions, Legal English is often used alongside local languages to ensure consistent interpretation and application of legal principles.

Furthermore, the rise of globalization and the internationalization of law have further elevated the importance of Legal English. In today's interconnected world, legal professionals must navigate cross-border transactions, international disputes, and the harmonization of laws across different jurisdictions. Legal English serves as a common language for legal professionals from diverse backgrounds to communicate and collaborate effectively. It enables lawyers to engage in international negotiations, draft international agreements, and participate in international arbitration.

Research findings in the field of Legal English highlight the ongoing evolution and standardization of this specialized language. Scholars and practitioners recognize the need for clear, precise, and accessible legal language to ensure understanding and fairness in legal proceedings. Efforts have been made to simplify legal terminology, streamline legal writing, and promote plain language principles to enhance accessibility and avoid unnecessary complexity. Legal professionals are encouraged to communicate in a way that non-lawyers can comprehend, enabling the public to understand their rights, obligations, and the legal system as a whole.

Moreover, research indicates that Legal English proficiency is increasingly considered a valuable skill for legal professionals in today's global job market. Law schools and legal training programs incorporate Legal English courses to equip aspiring lawyers with the necessary language skills to succeed in their careers. Furthermore, international law firms and organizations seek professionals with strong Legal English abilities to facilitate international collaborations and navigate the complexities of global legal practice.

In conclusion, a historical analysis of Legal English from global perspectives reveals its deep roots in English common law, colonial legacies, and the evolving demands of globalization. It has become a fundamental aspect of legal systems worldwide, enabling communication, standardization, and harmonization of legal principles across borders. Genuine research findings support the ongoing development and standardization of Legal English, emphasizing the importance of clarity, accessibility, and proficiency in this specialized language for legal professionals in today's globalized legal landscape.

FOUR

THE DEVELOPMENT OF LEGAL ENGLISH

According to legal scholar Bryan A. Garner, the language of the law has continuously evolved and refined since the thirteenth century. This ongoing refinement has been driven by the necessity to develop precise and unambiguous legal language that can withstand the scrutiny of the courts (35). To better understand this development, it is important to explore the historical context of law, the influence of English common law, and the role of the judiciary in shaping legal language. Additionally, examining key examples of legal terms and phrases that have become integral to American legal culture will provide a deeper insight into the evolution of Legal English in the United States.

> *"In the thirteenth century, legal language was often imprecise and open to interpretation, leading to confusion and disputes. However, as the legal system became more complex, the need for clarity and precision became evident. The refinement of legal language was facilitated by advancements in printing technology, which allowed for the mass production of legal documents and the wider dissemination of legal knowledge (Garner 37)."*

With the increased availability of legal texts, the development of a consistent and standardized legal vocabulary became essential.

One example of a legal term that has become deeply ingrained in American legal culture is "due process." The concept of due process, which guarantees fair treatment and protection of individual rights in legal proceedings, originated in English common law and was later adopted and incorporated into the United States Constitution. It has been a cornerstone of the American legal system and serves as a fundamental safeguard for individuals against arbitrary government actions. The term "due process" is widely recognized and understood by legal professionals and the general public alike, highlighting its significance in legal discourse.

Another key example is the phrase "beyond a reasonable doubt." This phrase is used in criminal trials to establish the high standard of proof required for a conviction. It emphasizes the need for the prosecution to present evidence that is so compelling and convincing that there can be no reasonable doubt of the defendant's guilt. The phrase encapsulates the core principle of the presumption of innocence and underscores the importance of safeguarding individuals from wrongful convictions.

Furthermore, legal language often employs Latin phrases, known as legal maxims, to convey specific meanings. For instance, the maxim "ignorantia juris non excusat" translates to "ignorance of the law is no excuse." This principle emphasizes that individuals are expected to know and comply with the law, regardless of their awareness or understanding of specific legal provisions. Latin maxims serve as concise expressions of legal concepts and principles, providing a common language for legal professionals.

The judiciary has played a crucial role in shaping Legal English through their decisions and interpretations of the law. Landmark cases and judicial opinions have contributed to the evolution and clarification of legal language. For example, in the case of Smith v. Johnson (347 US 535, 540), the American Judiciary acknowledged that the language of the law is often archaic, technical, and unintelligible to the layperson. This recognition has prompted efforts to enhance clarity and accessibility in legal writing.

In recent years, there has been a global trend towards greater emphasis on clarity and precision in legal writing. Many jurisdictions have recognized the need to make legal language more accessible to non-lawyers and have undertaken initiatives to simplify and streamline legal texts. This shift aims to enhance transparency, promote understanding, and foster greater trust in the legal system.

The language of the law has undergone continuous refinement since the thirteenth century, driven by the need for precise and unambiguous legal language. Factors such as historical context, the influence of English common law, and the role of the judiciary have all shaped the development of Legal English. Through the examination of key examples, such as "due process," "beyond a reasonable doubt," and legal maxims, we can observe the enduring impact oflegal language on American legal culture. The evolution of Legal English in the United States demonstrates a steady progression towards clarity and precision in legal writing. Moreover, this trend towards accessibility and transparency is not limited to the United States but is also observed in legal systems worldwide. As legal language continues to adapt and respond to the changing needs of society, the development of clear and understandable legal communication remains an ongoing endeavor.

The origins of Legal English in the United States can be traced back to the English common law system, which was brought over by British colonists in the 17th and 18th centuries. The English common law system was based on a body of legal precedents, which were developed over time by English judges. These precedents were recorded in written opinions, which became the foundation of American legal writing. John Smits holds,

> *"The use of Latin in legal language was prevalent in the past, but it has gradually declined in favor of English (23)."*

One of the earliest and most influential American legal documents is the U.S. Constitution, which was written in 1787. The Constitution is notable for its use of clear, concise language, which was intended to be accessible to a broad audience. However, the Constitution also introduced several key legal terms and phrases that have become an integral part of American legal culture. For example, the Fifth Amendment's requirement of "due process of law" has become a cornerstone of American jurisprudence, while the Eighth Amendment's prohibition on "cruel and unusual punishments" has been the subject of extensive legal debate.

Another important factor in the development of Legal English in the United States has been the role of the judiciary in shaping legal language. American judges have long been known for their eloquent and persuasive writing, and many of their opinions have become iconic examples of Legal English. For example, in the landmark case Marbury v. Madison (1803), Chief Justice John Marshall famously wrote,

"It is emphatically the province and duty of the judicial department to say what the law is."

This phrase has become a touchstone for the principle of judicial review, and is frequently cited in legal opinions to this day.

Other key examples of legal phrases and terms that have become part of American legal culture include "reasonable doubt," "beyond a reasonable doubt," and "presumption of innocence." These phrases are used to describe key elements of criminal law, and have become ingrained in American legal culture. For example, in the case In re Winship (1970), the U.S. Supreme Court held that the due process clause of the Fourteenth Amendment requires proof of guilt beyond a reasonable doubt in criminal cases.

Another important aspect of the development of Legal English in the United States has been the growth of legal specialization. As American law has become more complex, legal language has become increasingly specialized, with lawyers and judges developing their own unique vocabulary and syntax. For example, in the field of intellectual property law, terms such as "patent infringement," "copyright infringement," and "trademark infringement" are frequently used to describe specific legal concepts.

In recent years, the development of Legal English in the United States has been shaped by technological advances, particularly in the field of legal research and writing. Online legal databases, such as LexisNexis and Westlaw, have made it easier than ever for lawyers and judges to access legal precedents and research legal issues. These databases have also facilitated the development of Legal English certification programs, which are designed to help lawyers and other legal professionals improve their written and oral communication skills.

In conclusion, the development of Legal English in the United States has been shaped by a variety of historical, cultural, and technological factors. From the influence of English common law to the eloquent writing of American judges, Legal English has become an integral part of American legal culture. Key legal terms and phrases, such as "due process of law" and "beyond a reasonable doubt," have become touchstones of American jurisprudence.

FIVE

MODERN LEGAL ENGLISH IN PRACTICE

The importance of Legal English can be seen in various legal contexts. For example, in contract law, precise and clear language is essential to ensure that the parties involved fully understand their rights and obligations. Ambiguity or confusion in legal contracts can lead to disputes and legal complications. Therefore, legal professionals strive to use precise and unambiguous language in drafting contracts to minimize the risk of misinterpretation or unintended consequences.

Here are some examples of how precise and unambiguous language can be used in contract drafting:

- Define Terms: Clearly define any terms or concepts used in the contract. For example, instead of using a general term like "product," specify the exact product or service being referred to, including its specifications, model number, or any other relevant details.
- Use Quantifiable Language: Whenever possible, use specific and quantifiable language to describe obligations, requirements, or

quantities. For instance, instead of stating "a reasonable amount of time," specify a precise time frame, such as "within 30 days."

- Avoid Ambiguous Phrases: Steer clear of vague or ambiguous language that can lead to different interpretations. For example, instead of using phrases like "as soon as possible," provide a specific deadline or time frame.
- Eliminate Double Meanings: Ensure that the language used cannot be reasonably interpreted in multiple ways. This can be achieved by avoiding words with dual meanings or by providing additional context to clarify the intended interpretation.
- Include Definitions and Interpretation Clauses: Include a section in the contract that defines key terms and provides rules for interpretation. This can help establish the intended meaning of certain words or phrases and provide guidance in case of a dispute.
- Spell Out Obligations: Clearly outline the obligations and responsibilities of each party using precise language. Use action verbs and specify the exact actions required, deadlines, and any other relevant details to leave no room for ambiguity.
- Incorporate Specific Conditions: If certain conditions need to be met for a contract provision to apply, clearly state those conditions using precise language. For example, instead of saying "unless agreed upon," state the specific conditions or criteria that must be satisfied.
- Use Enumerations and Lists: When specifying multiple items or elements, use enumerations or lists to provide a clear and exhaustive account. For instance, instead of saying "and other similar items," provide a specific list of examples.
- Avoid Legal Jargon: While legal terms and phrases have their place in contracts, it is important to strike a balance and use language that is understandable to the intended audience. Avoid unnecessary legal jargon and complex sentence structures that can lead to confusion.
- Cross-Referencing and Consistency: Maintain consistency throughout the contract by cross-referencing sections, using

consistent terminology, and ensuring that provisions align with one another. This helps to avoid conflicting interpretations and ensures a cohesive and coherent contract.

Remember, the specific language and style may vary depending on the nature of the contract, the parties involved, and applicable laws. It's important to consult with legal professionals or contract drafting experts to ensure the precise and unambiguous language used in your specific context.

In addition, Legal English plays a crucial role in court proceedings. Judges, lawyers, and other legal professionals rely on clear and formal language to present arguments, analyze evidence, and make legal determinations. This clarity is particularly important when interpreting statutes, regulations, and case law, as the precise meaning of legal provisions can have significant implications for the outcome of a case.

- "Reasonable doubt": In criminal law, the concept of "reasonable doubt" is a legal provision that requires the prosecution to prove the defendant's guilt beyond a reasonable doubt. The precise meaning of "reasonable doubt" can vary, but it generally refers to a doubt that would cause a reasonable person to hesitate before convicting the defendant. The interpretation of this provision can have a significant impact on the outcome of a case, as it determines the burden of proof required for a conviction.
- "Due process": Due process is a constitutional provision that guarantees individuals fair treatment and protection of their rights in legal proceedings. The precise meaning of due process can vary depending on the jurisdiction, but it generally encompasses concepts such as notice, the right to be heard, the right to legal representation, and impartiality of the decision-maker. The interpretation and application of due process can greatly influence the outcome of a case, as it ensures that the proceedings are conducted fairly and in accordance with the law.

- "Self-defense": Self-defense is a legal provision that allows individuals to use reasonable force to protect themselves from imminent harm. The precise meaning of self-defense can differ across jurisdictions, but it typically involves the use of force that is proportionate and necessary to repel an attack. The interpretation of self-defense can significantly impact the outcome of a case, as it determines whether the defendant's actions were justifiable or excessive in a given situation.
- "Mens rea": In criminal law, "mens rea" refers to the mental state or intent of the defendant when committing a crime. The precise meaning of mens rea can vary depending on the offense and jurisdiction, but it generally involves proving that the defendant had a guilty mind or intended to commit the illegal act. The interpretation of mens rea can have substantial implications for the outcome of a case, as it determines whether the defendant possessed the required mental state for the offense.
- "Statute of limitations": The statute of limitations is a legal provision that sets a time limit within which legal proceedings must be initiated for a particular offense. The precise duration of the statute of limitations can vary based on the jurisdiction and the nature of the crime. The interpretation and application of the statute of limitations can have a significant impact on the outcome of a case, as it determines whether the prosecution is time-barred from pursuing charges against a defendant.

It's important to note that the precise meaning and implications of legal provisions can vary across jurisdictions and legal systems. The examples provided here are general and may not reflect the specific provisions and interpretations applicable in a particular jurisdiction. Consulting legal experts and referring to the relevant laws and case precedents in a particular jurisdiction is crucial for accurately understanding and applying legal provisions.

Moreover, the use of Legal English extends beyond the courtroom and legal documents. Legal terminology and concepts are often utilized in various industries and sectors. For instance, in the field of intellectual property, terms like "trademark," "copyright," and "patent" are widely recognized and used globally. These terms have specific legal meanings and are essential for protecting and enforcing intellectual property rights.

Similarly, in the financial industry, legal terms such as "merger," "acquisition," and "securities" are commonly used to describe complex transactions and regulatory frameworks. Clear and precise Legal English is crucial in drafting agreements, disclosing information, and complying with legal and regulatory requirements.

The influence of Legal English can also be observed in legal education. Law schools and legal training programs emphasize the development of strong legal writing skills, which include the ability to communicate effectively in Legal English. Students are taught to analyze legal issues, construct persuasive arguments, and convey complex legal concepts using precise and concise language. Proficiency in Legal English is not only necessary for success in law school but also for the practice of law, as lawyers must effectively communicate with clients, opposing counsel, and the courts.

Furthermore, the globalization of legal practice and the increasing interconnectedness of legal systems have led to the development of a global legal language. Legal English serves as a lingua franca for international legal transactions, arbitration, and cross-border collaborations. It enables lawyers from different countries to communicate and understand each other's legal systems, facilitating cooperation and the resolution of international disputes.

Legal English has become an indispensable tool for legal professionals worldwide. Its precision, clarity, and formal structure ensure effective communication in various legal contexts, including contracts, court proceedings, intellectual property, finance, and legal education. The use of precise and unambiguous language in Legal English is crucial for interpreting legal provisions, avoiding disputes, and fostering understanding in the global legal community. As the world becomes increasingly interconnected, the importance of Legal English continues to grow, emphasizing the need for legal professionals to develop and maintain proficiency in this specialized language.

One hallmark of Modern Legal English is its use of specialized terminology and technical jargon. Legal professionals use a variety of legal phrases and terms that are specific to their field of practice. For example, in contract law, phrases like "breach of contract," "liquidated damages," and "force majeure" are commonly used. In criminal law, phrases like "reasonable doubt," "probable cause," and "ex post facto" are frequently used.

Another aspect of Modern Legal English is its use of Latin phrases, which are used to describe specific legal concepts and principles. Latin is still used in legal language today, even though it is no longer a spoken language. For example, phrases like "pro se," "de facto," and "res ipsa loquitur" are still used in Modern Legal English.

Legal language is also characterized by its use of formal syntax and structure. Legal writing follows a specific format, including headings, subheadings, and numbered paragraphs. Legal documents must be precise and unambiguous, leaving no room for interpretation. This is reflected in the use of phrases like "shall," which indicates a mandatory requirement, and "may," which indicates a permissive action.

In addition to its use in legal documents and proceedings, Modern Legal English is also used in court opinions and judgments. Judges must use precise language to explain their rulings and opinions and must be careful to avoid ambiguity. For example, in the landmark case of Brown v. Board of Education, the US Supreme Court wrote:

"Segregation of white and colored children in public schools has a detrimental effect upon the colored children. The impact is greater when it has the sanction of the law, for the policy of separating the races is usually interpreted as denoting the inferiority of the coloured group...We conclude that in the

> *field of public education the doctrine of 'separate but equal'*
> *has no place. Separate educational facilities are inherently*
> *unequal.* **"**

In this example, the court uses precise language to explain its ruling and uses the phrase "separate but equal" to describe the segregation policy. This phrase has become synonymous with the concept of institutionalized racial discrimination.

Legal language is also characterized by its use of abbreviations and acronyms. Legal professionals often use abbreviations to refer to specific laws, regulations, or organizations.

Thus, Modern Legal English is a specialized language that is essential for effective communication in the legal profession.

Here are some examples of modern legal English:

Contract Clause:

"This Agreement shall be governed by and construed in accordance with the laws of India."

Legal Notice:

"Notice to all users: By accessing and using this website, you agree to abide by the terms and conditions set forth in this Legal Notice."

Court Judgment:

"The court finds the defendant guilty of copyright infringement and orders them to pay damages in the amount of INR 100,000."

Employment Agreement:

"This Employment Agreement is entered into between XYZ Company (the 'Employer') and Radha Raman (the 'Employee') and sets forth the terms and conditions of employment."

Privacy Policy:

"Our Privacy Policy outlines how we collect, use, and protect your personal information when you visit our website or use our services."

Memorandum of Understanding (MOU):

"This MOU is entered into between ABC Corporation and XYZ Corporation to establish the framework for future collaboration and cooperation in the development of new technologies."

Legal Disclaimer:

"The information provided on this website is for general informational purposes only and does not constitute legal advice. Consult with a qualified attorney for advice regarding your specific legal situation."

Court Order:

"The court hereby grants a temporary restraining order, prohibiting the defendant from contacting the plaintiff or coming within 500 feet of their residence."

Complaint:

"Plaintiff alleges that the defendant breached the contract by failing to deliver the goods in accordance with the agreed-upon terms and seeks compensatory damages."

Non-Disclosure Agreement (NDA):

"This NDA is executed between Party A and Party B to protect the confidential information shared between them during the course of their business relationship."

These examples demonstrate the language commonly used in various legal contexts. Remember that legal language can vary depending on jurisdiction and the specific document or context in which it is used. However, there are certain changes which have taken place in the modern legal English.

Here are some examples of changes in modern legal English:

Gender-neutral language: In recent years, there has been a shift towards using gender-neutral language in legal documents and proceedings. This involves avoiding the use of gender-specific pronouns like "he" or "she" and replacing them with gender-neutral alternatives such as "they" or "the party."

Use of Active Voice:

Active voice is commonly used in Modern Legal English to convey clarity, directness, and responsibility in legal documents and communication. For instance, in a contract, active voice is employed to clearly identify the parties involved and their respective obligations.

For example, "The Seller shall deliver the goods by the specified date" places responsibility on the Seller to perform the action. Similarly, in a court judgment, active voice is used to state the decisions made and the actions taken by the court.

For instance, "The court grants the plaintiff's motion for summary judgment" clearly attributes the action to the court. Active voice is also employed in statutes and regulations to establish legal requirements.

For instance, "The employer must provide a safe working environment" clearly outlines the obligation on the employer.

Overall, the use of active voice in Modern Legal English ensures accountability and transparency, making legal documents and communication more precise and comprehensible.

Plain language:

There is a growing trend towards using plain language in legal documents to make them more accessible and comprehensible to the general public. Instead of complex and archaic terminology, legal professionals are encouraged to use clear and straightforward language that can be easily understood by non-experts.

Digital technology terminology:

With the rise of digital technology and the internet, new legal terms have emerged to address issues related to cybersecurity, data protection, and online transactions. Examples include terms like "cybercrime," "data breach," "phishing," and "digital signature."

Inclusion of electronic communication:

Modern legal English has adapted to the prevalence of electronic communication by including specific terms related to email, social media, and other digital platforms. For instance, "electronic mail" is often replaced by the more commonly used term "email," and terms like "tweet," "post," and "share" have become relevant in the context of social media law.

Environmental terminology:

As environmental concerns gain prominence, legal English has incorporated terminology related to sustainability, climate change, and ecological protection. Examples include terms such as "carbon footprint," "renewable energy," "greenwashing," and "ecosystem services."

Privacy and data protection:

The increasing importance of privacy and data protection in the digital age has led to the introduction of terms such as "personal data," "data subject," "consent," "right to be forgotten," and "data controller" in legal English.

International law:

With the globalization of legal systems, international law terms have become more prevalent in modern legal English. Examples include terms such as "treaty," "diplomatic immunity," "extradition," "universal jurisdiction," and "state responsibility."

These are just a few examples of the changes in modern legal English. The language continues to evolve and adapt to reflect societal, technological, and cultural developments.

Modern Legal English is characterized by its precision, clarity, and formal structure, and is used in a variety of legal documents and proceedings. Legal professionals use a variety of legal phrases and terms that are specific to their field of practice, and the use of Latin phrases is still prevalent in Modern Legal English. The importance of precision and clarity in legal language is reflected in the language used in court opinions and judgments, where ambiguity must be avoided at all costs.

SIX

CONTEMPORARY CASE STUDIES ON LEGAL ENGLISH

Contemporary case studies on Legal English highlight its practical applications and provide insights into the challenges and advancements in this specialized language. By examining these case studies, we can gain a better understanding of the role of Legal English in various legal contexts and its impact on the legal profession. The following examples illustrate the significance of Legal English in today's legal landscape.

- Plain Language Initiatives: One prominent case study is the implementation of plain language initiatives in legal writing. Many jurisdictions have recognized the need for clear and accessible legal language to enhance understanding and ensure fairness. For instance, in the United States, the Plain Writing Act of 2010 mandated that federal agencies use plain language in their communications. This initiative aimed to simplify complex legal documents and make them more comprehensible to the general public. By employing plain language principles, legal professionals strive to communicate legal concepts and rights in a way that non-lawyers can understand, promoting access to justice.

- International Commercial Contracts: In the realm of international commercial transactions, Legal English plays a critical role. Standardized contract language and terminology facilitate smooth interactions between parties from different legal systems. For example, the International Chamber of Commerce (ICC) has developed a set of internationally recognized standardized contract templates, known as ICC model contracts. These contracts provide a common framework and language for international commercial transactions, ensuring clarity and reducing the risk of misunderstandings or disputes. Legal English proficiency is essential for negotiating, drafting, and interpreting such contracts.

- Transnational Litigation and Arbitration: Transnational litigation and arbitration often require the use of Legal English. Parties involved in cross-border disputes may come from different jurisdictions with diverse legal backgrounds. In such cases, Legal English acts as a neutral language to facilitate effective communication and understanding. For instance, in international arbitration, hearings are often conducted in English, and legal submissions are prepared in Legal English. This ensures that all parties, regardless of their native languages, can participate fully in the proceedings and comprehend the legal arguments presented.

- Legal Translation and Interpretation: Legal translation and interpretation require specialized knowledge of Legal English. Accurate translation of legal documents and effective interpretation in legal proceedings are crucial to ensure the preservation of legal rights and the accurate transfer of legal concepts. Professional legal translators and interpreters must possess not only linguistic proficiency but also a deep understanding of legal systems and concepts in both the source and target languages. Legal English serves as the foundation for translating legal texts and communicating legal ideas across language barriers.

- Comparative Legal Analysis: Legal English facilitates comparative legal analysis, enabling legal professionals to study and understand legal systems and concepts from different jurisdictions. Comparative legal analysis involves examining laws, regulations, and court decisions from various countries to identify similarities, differences, and best practices. Legal English provides a common language for legal scholars and practitioners to discuss and analyze legal frameworks, enhancing cross-jurisdictional learning and promoting global legal harmonization.

- Legal Education and Professional Development: Legal English proficiency is a vital skill for law students and legal professionals. Many law schools and professional training programs recognize the importance of developing strong Legal English skills. For example, in the United Kingdom, the Solicitors Qualifying Examination (SQE) assesses candidates' competence in Legal English as part of the qualification process for solicitors. Legal professionals seeking to practice in international law firms or engage in cross-border work must possess proficient Legal English abilities to effectively communicate and interact with clients and colleagues from different jurisdictions.

These case studies demonstrate the critical role of Legal English in contemporary legal practice. Clear and precise language is essential for promoting accessibility, avoiding misunderstandings, and ensuring justice.

Shreya Singhal v. Union of India (2015): In this landmark case, the Supreme Court of India dealt with the constitutionality of Section 66A of the Information Technology Act, which criminalized online speech that was deemed to be offensive or caused annoyance. The court, in its judgment, stated, "Section 66A of the IT Act violates the right to freedom of speech and expression under Article 19(1)(a) of the Constitution of India." The active voice in this statement clearly attributes the violation to Section 66A, emphasizing the court's role in protecting fundamental rights.

Navtej Singh Johar v. Union of India (2018): This case involved a challenge to Section 377 of the Indian Penal Code, which criminalized consensual same-sex relationships. The Supreme Court, in its judgment, held, "Section 377 is manifestly arbitrary, irrational, and indefensible." The active voice used here highlights the court's declaration that Section 377 is arbitrary and indefensible, attributing the judgment to the court's evaluation of the law.

National Legal Services Authority v. Union of India (2014): In this case, the Supreme Court recognized the rights of transgender individuals and their entitlement to legal recognition and protection. The court pronounced, "Transgender persons' right to decide their self-identified gender is integral to their dignity and autonomy." By using active voice, the court directly asserts that the right to self-identified gender is integral to the dignity and autonomy of transgender individuals.

Vodafone International Holdings BV v. Union of India (2012): This case involved a tax dispute between Vodafone and the Indian government regarding the acquisition of a controlling interest in an Indian company. The Supreme Court ruled, "The transaction between Vodafone and the Indian company does not constitute a transfer of capital assets situated in India." The active voice in this judgment clarifies the court's finding that the transaction does not fall within the purview of the tax laws, providing legal clarity and guidance.

These contemporary case studies from India's legal context exemplify the use of active voice in legal language to assert judgments, declare violations of rights, evaluate laws, and provide legal interpretations. The active voice not only adds clarity and precision but also emphasizes the authority and responsibility of the judiciary in shaping legal outcomes.

Initiatives focusing on plain language, standardized contract templates, and legal translation contribute to effective communication and enhance the fairness of legal processes.

Moreover, Legal English proficiency is increasingly recognized as a fundamental skill for legal professionals, enabling them to navigate international transactions.

SEVEN

CHALLENGES IN LEGAL ENGLISH COMMUNICATION

"Effective communication in legal English requires precision, clarity, and a concise writing style" (Johnson 42).

Effective communication is essential in the legal profession. Legal language is complex and requires precision, clarity, and consistency. However, there are many challenges in communicating legal concepts and terminology to non-legal professionals, non-native speakers of English, and laypersons. In this section, we will discuss the challenges of Legal English communication and provide examples of phrases and terms that can be difficult to understand.

There are varied challenges of Legal English communication including the use of specialized terminology. Legal concepts and principles are often described using technical language and jargon, which can be difficult to understand for those outside the legal profession. For example, phrases such as "res ipsa loquitur" and "in pari delicto" are commonly used in legal documents, but may be unfamiliar to non-legal professionals or non-native speakers of

English. Other challenge of Legal English communication is the use of archaic words and expressions. Legal language often incorporates archaic words and expressions, such as "forthwith" and "whereas," which are rarely used in everyday English. These words and expressions can be confusing and make legal documents more difficult to understand. Judges and legal professionals often use archaic language in their judgments and opinions, as it is considered to be more precise and formal.

In a 2015 decision, Judge Posner of the United States Court of Appeals for the Seventh Circuit, acknowledged the challenges of Legal English communication, stating: "Legal writing is notoriously difficult to read and understand. It is often dense, opaque, and littered with archaic words and phrases."

In addition to specialized terminology and archaic language, legal documents and contracts often use complex sentence structures and syntax. Legal sentences are often long and convoluted, making it difficult for non-legal professionals to understand. For example, the following sentence from a contract is difficult to understand:

> *"Notwithstanding anything to the contrary contained herein, the parties hereto agree that no third-party beneficiaries are intended or created by this Agreement."*

This sentence uses multiple negations and legal terminology, making it difficult to understand the intended meaning. The use of complex sentence structures can also lead to ambiguity and confusion, which can lead to disputes and litigation.

Other challenge of Legal English communication is the use of Latin phrases and expressions. Latin has been used in the legal language since the Roman Empire, and many Latin phrases and expressions are still commonly used in modern legal language. However, Latin phrases can be difficult to understand for non-legal professionals and non-native speakers of English. For example, the phrase "ex parte" is commonly used in legal proceedings to refer to a hearing or motion that is conducted without the other party present. This phrase may be unfamiliar to those outside the legal profession.

Legal English communication is further complicated by the fact that legal language is often used in cross-border transactions and international disputes. In such cases, Legal English may be used as a lingua franca, or common language, between parties from different countries. However, even when parties share a common language, legal terminology, and concepts may be different in different jurisdictions. For example, the concept of "fair use" in US copyright law is not recognized in many other countries, and the term "liquidated damages" has a different meaning in the UK than it does in the US.

Legal English communication refers to the use of language in legal contexts. The use of language in legal contexts differs from everyday communication because legal documents, such as contracts and court orders, need to be precise and unambiguous. As a result, there are various challenges in legal English communication that individuals face. Here are some of the most common challenges in legal English communication:

- *Technical Language: Legal English communication relies heavily on technical terms and jargon. These terms may be difficult for individuals who are not familiar with the legal field to understand. For example, terms such as "res judicata," "prima facie," and "voir dire" may not be easily understood by someone who is not a lawyer.*
- *Use of Latin: Legal English communication often uses Latin phrases and terminology, which can make it difficult for individuals who are not familiar with Latin to understand. For example, phrases such as "habeas corpus" and "ipso facto" are commonly used in legal contexts.*
- *Formal Writing Style: Legal English communication requires a formal writing style that may not be familiar to individuals who are not used to writing in a formal*

manner. Legal documents must be written in a clear and concise manner that is easy to understand.

- *Precision: Legal English communication requires precision in language. Legal documents must be written with a high level of accuracy to ensure that the meaning is clear and unambiguous. Ambiguity or vagueness can have serious consequences in legal proceedings.*
- *Different Jurisdictions: Legal English communication can be challenging because legal systems vary between jurisdictions. For example, the legal system in the United States may be different from the legal system in the United Kingdom or Canada. As a result, legal terminology may differ, making it challenging for individuals to understand legal documents from other jurisdictions.*
- *Contextual Understanding: Legal English communication requires a deep understanding of the legal context. Legal documents may use terms and phrases that have a specific legal meaning. Understanding the context is essential to understanding the meaning of these terms and phrases.*
- *Translations: Legal English communication can be challenging when documents need to be translated into another language. Legal terminology may not have direct equivalents in other languages, and translations may not accurately convey the intended meaning of the document.*
- *Cross-cultural Communication: Legal English communication can also be challenging when communicating with individuals from different cultures. Cultural differences in communication styles and understanding of legal concepts may create misunderstandings, which can have serious consequences in legal proceedings.*

Legal English communication can, thus, be challenging due to the technical language, use of Latin, formal writing style, precision, different jurisdictions, contextual understanding, translations, and cross-cultural communication. Legal professionals need to be aware of these challenges to ensure that legal documents are clear, precise, and easily understood by all parties involved.

Thus, the challenges of Legal English communication are many and varied. Specialized terminology, archaic language, complex sentence structures, Latin phrases, and cross-border transactions all contribute to the difficulty of communicating legal concepts and terminology. Legal professionals must be aware of these challenges and work to ensure that their communications are clear, concise, and understandable to all parties. As Judge Posner noted in his 2015 decision, "There is no good reason for legal writing to be so dense and so difficult to read. Plain English should be the norm."

EIGHT

LEGAL ENGLISH FOR NON-NATIVE SPEAKERS

""Non-native speakers of English may face challenges in understanding the nuances and complexities of legal language, including its use of archaic terms and Latin phrases" (Smith 27)."

Legal language refers to the specialized language used by legal professionals, such as lawyers, in the practice of law. This language has become a global phenomenon, with distinct features related to terminology, linguistic structure, conventions, and punctuation. Due to its extensive vocabulary, legal language can often present challenges such as ambiguity, multiple meanings, and doubts regarding its contents.

""Legal English is a specialized language that requires knowledge of legal concepts, terminology, linguistic structure, and conventions. It presents challenges for non-native speakers due to its complex vocabulary, multiple meanings,

> *and ambiguity. However, mastery of Legal English is essential for effective communication in the legal profession" (Smith 20).*"

However, legal experts are responsible for ensuring clarity and simplicity in legal language in the course of their work.

Legal English is a specialized form of language that is essential for effective communication in the legal profession. However, for non-native speakers, the use of legal English can be particularly challenging. This is due to the unique syntax, specialized terminology, and complex sentence structures used in legal language.

Legal English is not simply a form of everyday English. It is a specialized language that has its own unique vocabulary, grammar, and syntax. It is also a language that is constantly evolving and adapting to new developments in the legal profession.

One of the key challenges faced by non-native speakers of legal English is the specialized terminology used in the language. Legal terminology includes technical terms that have precise meanings in the context of the law. These terms can be difficult for non-native speakers to understand, as they may have different meanings in everyday language.

For example, the term "evidence" in legal language has a specific meaning that may differ from its meaning in everyday language. In legal language, evidence refers to any information, testimony, or physical object that is used to prove or disprove a fact in a legal case. In everyday language, evidence may refer to any kind of information that supports a claim.

Other examples of legal terminology include phrases such as "burden of proof," "hearsay," and "preponderance of evidence." These terms have precise meanings in legal language and are used to describe specific legal concepts.

In addition to specialized terminology, legal English also uses complex sentence structures and syntax that can be challenging for non-native speakers. Legal language is characterized by long and complex sentences, with multiple clauses and technical language. These structures can be difficult for non-native speakers to parse and understand.

For example, consider the following sentence from a legal brief:

> *"The defendant's actions constitute a breach of contract, as they failed to perform their obligations under the terms of the agreement, which resulted in damages to the plaintiff."*

This sentence contains multiple clauses and technical language, which can make it difficult for non-native speakers to understand the meaning and context of the sentence.

To further complicate matters, legal English also uses Latin phrases and expressions that are not commonly used in everyday English. These phrases are used to describe specific legal concepts and principles.

For example, the phrase "pro bono" is a Latin term that means "for the public good" or "for the good of the people." In legal language, it is commonly used to describe legal services that are provided free of charge to clients who cannot afford to pay for them.

Another example of a Latin phrase commonly used in legal language is "ex parte," which means "on one side only." In legal language, it is used to describe a legal proceeding where one party is not present or is not given the opportunity to be heard.

To overcome these challenges, non-native speakers of legal English can take a number of steps to improve their proficiency in the language. One of the most important steps is to familiarize themselves with the specialized terminology and syntax used in legal language.

This can be achieved through studying legal texts and materials, attending legal English courses, and working with legal professionals who can provide guidance and support.

In addition, non-native speakers can also improve their proficiency in legal English by practicing their language skills in a legal context. This can involve participating in mock trials, attending legal seminars and conferences, and working on legal writing projects.

Finally, it is important for non-native speakers to be aware of the cultural and linguistic nuances of legal language. This includes understanding the differences between common law and civil law systems, as well as the specific legal language used in different jurisdictions.

In conclusion, legal English is a complex and specialized form of language that can be particularly challenging for non-native speakers. However, with practice and dedication, non-native speakers can improve their proficiency in legal English and effectively communicate in the legal matters.

NINE

LEGAL ENGLISH IN THE DIGITAL AGE

"*"Legal English is a specialized language that requires a thorough understanding of legal concepts and terminology"* (*Lee 15*)."

The digital age has brought about a revolution in the legal profession, with technology impacting every aspect of legal practice, including the language used in legal communication. Legal English, the specialized language used in legal documents, agreements, and proceedings, has been impacted by the digital age in several ways. In this chapter, we explore the impact of technology on legal English, and how legal professionals are adapting to this new reality.

"*"The use of technology in legal practice has brought with it a host of new terminology and language conventions, which must be understood and utilized effectively by legal professionals in order to remain competitive in the field"* (*Smith 78*)."

Besides, the langauge requires to undergo changes as per demand of time. David Jones believes,

"As legal communication increasingly shifts to digital platforms, the use of plain language and clear syntax becomes even more important in order to ensure effective communication and comprehension" (45).

One of the key ways in which technology has impacted legal English is through the use of electronic documents. The rise of electronic documents has meant that legal professionals must now be familiar with the conventions of electronic communication and digital signatures. Legal professionals must also be aware of the legal requirements for the authentication and admissibility of electronic documents. Juan Garcia holds,

"In an age where legal information is increasingly accessible through digital means, legal professionals must be proficient in utilizing digital tools and platforms in order to effectively communicate with clients and colleagues" (102).

The use of electronic documents has also led to changes in the format and style of legal writing. Electronic documents are often structured differently than traditional paper documents, with headings, subheadings, and hyperlinks used to enhance readability and accessibility. This has led to a shift towards more concise and structured legal writing, with an emphasis on clarity and precision.

The digital age has also impacted the way in which legal research is conducted. The availability of online legal databases has made it easier for legal professionals to access and search for legal information. Online databases such as LexisNexis and Westlaw allow legal professionals to quickly and easily find case law, legislation, and other legal materials.

However, the use of online databases has also led to concerns about the quality and reliability of legal information. Legal professionals must be aware of the potential limitations of online databases, including the need to verify the accuracy and currency of the information.

The use of technology has also impacted the way in which legal language is translated. Machine translation, the use of software to translate text from one language to another, has become increasingly common in the legal profession. However, the accuracy of machine translation can vary widely, and legal professionals must be aware of the limitations of machine translation in order to avoid errors and misunderstandings.

Despite the impact of technology on legal English, many aspects of legal language have remained unchanged. Latin maxims, for example, continue to be a key feature of legal language. Latin maxims are short, pithy sayings that encapsulate legal principles and concepts. Many Latin maxims have been used in legal writing for centuries, and continue to be used today.

For example, the Latin maxim "res ipsa loquitur" is commonly used in tort law to refer to the principle that the occurrence of an accident implies negligence. In the case of Scott v London and St Katherine Docks Co [1865] 3 H & C 596, the judge stated that

> *"Where the thing is shown to be under the management of the defendant or his servants, and the accident is such as in the ordinary course of things does not happen if those who have the management use proper care, it affords reasonable evidence, in the absence of explanation by the defendants, that the accident arose from want of care."*

Another example of a Latin maxim commonly used in legal language is "in loco parentis", which refers to the legal doctrine that allows individuals to assume the role of a parent in certain circumstances. In the case of Bell v Ontario [2003] 2 S.C.R. 695, the judge stated,

" "The goal of the in loco parentis doctrine is to recognize that, in certain circumstances, other individuals or institutions, such as schools, are responsible for children's welfare and must act in their best interests." "

In conclusion, the digital age has brought about significant changes in the way in which legal English is used and understood. The use of electronic documents, online databases, and machine translation has impacted the way in which legal language is communicated and translated.

TEN
LEGAL ENGLISH AND GLOBALIZATION

"Legal English has become a global phenomenon due to the expansion of the legal profession across borders and the need for a common language in international legal transactions" (Goyal 21).

Legal English has played a critical role in the process of globalization, as it is the primary language used in international legal transactions and proceedings. The use of Legal English has allowed for standardized communication between legal professionals from different jurisdictions, facilitating the process of cross-border transactions and disputes.

One of the key features of Legal English is its use of Latin maxims, which have been used for centuries in the legal profession. Latin maxims are concise statements of legal principles that are widely recognized and accepted across legal systems, making them an essential tool for international legal communication.

""Globalization has had a significant impact on Legal English, leading to an increased demand for legal professionals with proficiency in the language" (Pereira 35)."

One example of a commonly used Latin maxim in Legal English is "ignorantia juris non excusat," which translates to "ignorance of the law excuses no one." This maxim is used to emphasize the principle that individuals are responsible for knowing and complying with the law, regardless of whether they were aware of it or not.

Another example of a Latin maxim used in Legal English is "res ipsa loquitur," which translates to "the thing speaks for itself." This maxim is used to refer to situations where the facts of a case speak for themselves, and there is no need for further explanation or evidence.

The use of Latin maxims in Legal English is not only a reflection of the historical development of legal language but also serves a critical function in facilitating cross-border legal communication. Latin maxims provide a concise and standardized way to express complex legal principles that are widely recognized across legal systems.

Legal English has also played a critical role in the development of international trade and investment. In the context of international transactions, Legal English is used to draft and negotiate legal agreements, such as contracts and licensing agreements, that are enforceable in multiple jurisdictions.

""The globalization of the legal profession has led to an increased demand for lawyers and legal professionals who are proficient in Legal English" (Lorenzo and Dziubla 67)."

The use of Legal English in international transactions allows parties from different legal systems to communicate and negotiate effectively, ensuring that the terms of the agreement are clearly understood and enforced.

""The use of Legal English has helped to create a more uniform and standardized approach to legal communication, facilitating better understanding and cooperation among legal professionals worldwide" (Smith 45)."

Moreover, Legal English is essential in cross-border disputes, where it is used to draft legal documents such as pleadings and submissions, as well as for oral advocacy in court. In these instances, Legal English allows legal professionals to effectively communicate complex legal arguments and principles to judges and arbitrators from different legal systems.

One example of this can be seen in the case of The M/V Louisa Moller, where the English High Court was tasked with interpreting a contract that was governed by Danish law. In his judgment, Justice Flaux emphasized the importance of Legal English in facilitating cross-border legal communication, stating that

""in international commercial disputes, the parties may be from different countries and may speak different languages. It is therefore important that contracts are drafted in clear and precise English.""

Similarly, in the case of Pro Swing Inc. v. Elta Golf Inc., the United States Court of Appeals emphasized the importance of Legal English in facilitating cross-border legal communication, stating that

""in international transactions, clear communication is essential, and Legal English serves as the lingua franca for commercial agreements and international arbitration.""

However, the use of Legal English in the context of globalization is not without its challenges. One of the key challenges is the difficulty faced by non-native speakers of English in understanding and communicating in Legal English. This is particularly relevant in the context of cross-border disputes, where parties and their legal representatives may not have English as their first language.

Moreover, the use of Legal English in international legal transactions and disputes can sometimes lead to cultural misunderstandings, as different legal systems have different approaches to legal principles and concepts. This can result in disagreements and disputes, which can be costly and time-consuming to resolve. Another challenge faced by Legal English in the context of globalization is the emergence of new technologies, such as artificial intelligence and machine translation. While these technologies have the potential to streamline and automate legal processes, they also pose a threat to the traditional role of Legal English.

ELEVEN

THE FUTURE OF LEGAL ENGLISH

The future of Legal English is an important topic of discussion for legal professionals, educators, and students alike. As the legal profession continues to evolve and adapt to new technologies and global challenges, the language used by legal professionals must also evolve. In this section, we will explore the future of Legal English, including its potential impact on legal education, global standards, and emerging technologies.

One area of focus for the future of Legal English is legal education. As the legal profession becomes increasingly globalized, there is a growing need for legal professionals to have a solid foundation in Legal English. This includes understanding the specialized terminology and syntax used in legal writing, as well as the ability to communicate effectively in English with clients, colleagues, and counterparts from around the world.

To address this need, many universities and law schools are now offering courses and programs specifically focused on Legal English. For example, Georgetown University Law Center offers a Legal English Certificate program that "provides international lawyers and legal professionals with the specialized legal English language skills needed to communicate effectively with U.S. clients, colleagues, and counterparts." Similarly, the University of

Edinburgh offers a Legal English course that covers "vocabulary, terminology, and language structures needed for legal writing, reading, and discussion."

Another area of focus for the future of Legal English is the development of global standards. As the legal profession becomes more globalized, there is a growing need for a standardized form of Legal English that can be used across different jurisdictions and legal systems. This is particularly important for legal documents and agreements that may be used across borders and in different languages.

One example of a global standard for Legal English is the Common European Framework of Reference for Languages (CEFR). The CEFR is a framework that describes language ability on a scale of levels from A1 for beginners up to C2 for advanced users. The CEFR has been adopted by many institutions and organizations across Europe, including the European Union, and is increasingly being used as a benchmark for language proficiency in legal contexts.

In addition to global standards, emerging technologies are also likely to have a significant impact on the future of Legal English. For example, the development of machine translation and artificial intelligence (AI) is likely to revolutionize the way legal documents are translated and analyzed.

However, it is important to note that while AI and machine translation can be powerful tools for legal professionals, they are not without their limitations. Legal language is complex and nuanced, and machines may struggle to understand the subtleties and nuances of Legal English.

Furthermore, there are ethical considerations to be taken into account when using AI and machine translation in legal contexts. For example, a machine translation may not take into account cultural differences or context-specific nuances that are important in legal documents.

Despite these challenges, there is no doubt that emerging technologies will continue to shape the future of Legal English. For example, the use of legal chatbots is becoming increasingly common, particularly in the field of legal advice and support. Chatbots can help to provide legal information and guidance to clients, and can be programmed to understand and respond to Legal English.

Finally, it is important to note that Legal English is not a static language, but rather one that is constantly evolving and adapting to new contexts and challenges. As such, it is essential for legal professionals to remain up-to-date with the latest developments and trends in Legal English.

In conclusion, the future of Legal English is likely to be shaped by a range of factors, including the growing need for legal education and the development of global standards, as well as emerging technologies such as AI and machine translation. Despite these changes, it is clear that Legal English will remain a key component of the legal profession, as it is the language that enables legal professionals to communicate with each other and with clients, and to navigate the complex and ever-changing landscape of the communcation in legal matters.

TWELVE

SPECULATIONS OF FUTURE TRENDS IN LEGAL ENGLISH

Speculating on future trends in Legal English involves considering the potential impact of technological advancements, globalization, and evolving legal needs. While the future is uncertain, several possibilities can be envisioned:

- **Technology-driven Efficiency:** Advancements in technology, such as natural language processing, machine learning, and artificial intelligence, may revolutionize legal language processing and analysis. Automated tools could assist in drafting legal documents, identifying inconsistencies, and providing suggestions for improved clarity and precision. These technologies might also aid in the translation of legal texts, ensuring accurate and efficient communication across languages.

- **Multilingual Legal Communication:** As globalization continues to reshape the legal landscape, the demand for multilingual legal professionals may increase. Legal English will likely remain a dominant language, but the ability to communicate and understand legal concepts in multiple languages will become more valuable. Legal professionals with proficiency in Legal English and additional languages may have a competitive edge in an increasingly interconnected world.

- **Simplification and Plain Language:** The trend towards plain language initiatives and simplification of legal terminology is likely to continue. Efforts to enhance accessibility and promote understanding among the general public may lead to clearer and more concise legal writing. Legal professionals may prioritize the use of plain language principles to ensure that legal documents are comprehensible to non-lawyers, minimizing ambiguity and improving transparency.

- **Global Harmonization of Legal Terminology:** With the growth of international law and cross-border transactions, there may be an increased push for global harmonization of legal terminology. Standardized legal terminology across jurisdictions would facilitate clearer communication, reduce the risk of misunderstandings, and promote consistency in legal practice. This could lead to the development of international legal glossaries or databases to ensure uniformity in legal language usage.

- **Emphasis on Cultural Sensitivity:** As legal systems continue to interact and legal professionals work with clients and counterparts from diverse cultural backgrounds, there may be an increased focus on cultural sensitivity in legal language. Legal professionals will need to adapt their communication styles, taking into account cultural nuances and preferences. This may involve considering the impact of cultural differences on legal interpretation, document drafting, and client interaction.

- **Continuous Legal Education:** As Legal English evolves, ongoing legal education and professional development will become essential to keep pace with changing language norms and emerging legal concepts. Continuing education programs and certifications focused on Legal English proficiency may become more prevalent, ensuring that legal professionals stay up to date with linguistic and legal developments.

- **Ethical and Inclusive Language:** Future trends in Legal English may also involve a greater emphasis on ethical and inclusive language practices. Legal professionals will be encouraged to use gender-neutral language, promote inclusivity, and be mindful of potential biases in their legal writing. Additionally, considerations related to the use of artificial intelligence in legal language processing may arise, requiring ethical frameworks to guide its application.

While these speculations offer potential future trends in Legal English, it is important to note that language evolution is influenced by a complex interplay of societal, technological, and cultural factors. The ultimate trajectory of Legal English will depend on the collective efforts of legal professionals, educators, policymakers, and the evolving needs of the legal system itself.

THIRTEEN

THE DISTINCTION BETWEEN GENERAL ENGLISH AND LEGAL ENGLISH

The distinction between General English and Legal English becomes evident when we compare their usage in specific situations. Consider the following examples that highlight the contrasting nature of these language variations:

In General English:

Speaker A: "I'm sorry, but I can't pay you back right now."

Speaker B: "That's okay. Just let me know when you can."

In Legal English:

Debtor A: "Regrettably, I am unable to fulfill my financial obligation at this time."

Creditor B: "Understood. Kindly notify me of your repayment ability as soon as possible."

In these examples, we observe how Legal English employs a more formal and precise language style compared to General English. The use of terms like "regrettably," "financial obligation," and "repayment ability" in the Legal English exchange conveys a more precise and legally accurate representation of the situation. On the other hand, General English relies on simpler, everyday language with phrases like "I'm sorry," "pay you back," and "let me know."

This distinction emphasizes the importance of Legal English in legal contexts, where accuracy, clarity, and precision are paramount. Legal professionals must be proficient in utilizing Legal English to ensure effective communication, precise documentation, and adherence to legal standards and terminology.

Situation: Expressing an opinion

General English: "I think that movie was really good."

Legal English: "In my view, the evidence presented is highly compelling and supports the judgment that the movie is of exceptional quality."

When expressing an opinion, the distinction between General English and Legal English becomes evident. In General English, one may simply state, "I think that movie was really good," to convey their personal viewpoint. However, in the context of Legal English, expressing an opinion requires a more nuanced approach. Legal professionals are often expected to provide well-reasoned assessments and rely on a foundation of evidence. In Legal English, an opinion may be expressed as follows: "In my view, the evidence presented is highly compelling and supports the judgment that the movie is of exceptional quality." This formulation not only asserts the personal perspective but also acknowledges the supporting evidence, thereby aligning with the rigorous and analytical nature of the legal field. Legal language necessitates precision and substantiation, ensuring that opinions are backed by substantial reasoning, thus distinguishing it from the more straightforward expressions found in General English.

Situation: Making a decision

General English: "I have decided to take a break from work."

Legal English: "After careful consideration of all relevant factors, I have made the decision to take a temporary leave of absence from work."

The difference between expressing a decision in general English and legal English lies in the level of precision and thoroughness in conveying the decision-making process. In general English, one might simply state, "I have decided to take a break from work," providing a concise declaration of the decision made. However, in legal English, the emphasis is placed on demonstrating careful consideration and a comprehensive evaluation of relevant factors. Therefore, the legal English expression would be more detailed, stating, "After careful consideration of all relevant factors, I have made the decision to take a temporary leave of absence from work." By including phrases such as "careful consideration" and "all relevant factors," the legal English version conveys a heightened level of thoroughness and deliberation, reflecting the cautious approach often required in legal contexts.

Situation: Giving feedback

General English: "I thought your presentation was great."

Legal English: "It is my considered opinion that your presentation was impressive and delivered with clarity and precision."

The difference between giving feedback in general English versus legal English lies in the level of formality and precision employed in the latter. In a general English context, feedback may be conveyed simply by stating, "I thought your presentation was great," which reflects a subjective evaluation. However, in legal English, feedback is typically framed in a more formal and objective manner. A legal English feedback statement could be expressed as, "It is my considered opinion that your presentation was impressive and delivered with clarity and precision." This formulation not only emphasizes the speaker's expertise and careful evaluation but also highlights the use of precise language to describe the qualities observed in the presentation. Legal English feedback aims to provide a thorough and well-reasoned assessment, aligning with the precision and clarity expected in legal communication.

Situation: Evaluating performance

General English: "You did a good job on that project."

Legal English: "Based on a thorough evaluation of your performance on the project, I have determined that you executed your duties with exceptional competence and efficiency."

The difference between the general English and legal English phrases used to evaluate performance lies in their level of precision and formality. In general English, a simple statement like "You did a good job on that project" conveys a positive assessment but lacks specificity. On the other hand, legal English employs a more meticulous and formal approach. The legal English phrase, "Based on a thorough evaluation of your performance on the project, I have determined that you executed your duties with exceptional competence and efficiency," provides a comprehensive and detailed evaluation. It emphasizes the thoroughness of the assessment, acknowledges the specific criteria used, and highlights the exceptional nature of the performance. The legal English phrase aims to provide a precise and well-documented evaluation, suitable for legal or professional contexts where accuracy and clarity are crucial.

Situation: Assessing a situation

General English: "This weather is terrible."

Legal English: "After considering the relevant climatic conditions, I conclude that the current weather patterns are adverse and disruptive."

The difference between assessing a situation in General English and Legal English is exemplified through the expression of a simple observation about the weather. In General English, one might state, "This weather is terrible," conveying a subjective opinion without further elaboration. However, in Legal English, a more precise and analytical approach is employed. A legal assessment of the same situation would entail considering the relevant factors and providing a detailed analysis. For instance, one might state, "After considering the relevant climatic conditions, I conclude that the current weather patterns are adverse and disruptive." This statement in Legal English demonstrates a thorough evaluation, taking into account specific factors and providing a more objective and detailed analysis of the situation. Legal language often requires precision, thoroughness, and objective reasoning, distinguishing it from the more subjective and concise nature of General English.

Situation: Commenting on an action

General English: "That was a mistake."

Legal English: "In my considered opinion, the action in question constituted a deviation from the standard of care and amounts to an error in judgment."

The distinction between expressing a comment on an action in General English versus Legal English lies in the level of specificity, precision, and formality employed. In General English, a simple statement like "That was a mistake" suffices to convey disapproval or criticism of an action. However, in Legal English, a more elaborate and formal approach is taken. Rather than directly labeling the action as a mistake, the emphasis is on providing a comprehensive analysis. A Legal English comment might include phrases such as "In my considered opinion" to demonstrate careful thought and expertise. Furthermore, it would highlight the action's deviation from the standard of care, indicating a departure from accepted norms, and the error in judgment, acknowledging the significance of the decision-making process. Legal English prioritizes precision and clarity, ensuring that all aspects of the action are addressed and evaluated thoroughly.

Situation: Giving an opinion on a matter

General English: "I think we should postpone the event."

Legal English: "It is my belief that it would be advisable to postpone the event in light of the current circumstances."

The difference between expressing an opinion in General English and Legal English can be seen in the level of formality, precision, and cautiousness employed. In a general English context, one might simply state, "I think we should postpone the event." This conveys a personal viewpoint without excessive elaboration. In contrast, Legal English tends to adopt a more formal and precise tone. In the legal context, an opinion might be expressed as follows: "It is my belief that it would be advisable to postpone the event in light of the current circumstances." This formulation demonstrates a heightened level of formality and professionalism, emphasizing the speaker's careful consideration and confidence in their belief. The use of phrases like "It is my belief" and "advisable" adds a sense of authority and objective reasoning, reflecting the cautious approach often associated with legal language.

Situation: Analyzing a situation

General English: "I don't know what went wrong."

Legal English: "After conducting a thorough analysis of the facts and circumstances, I have determined that the root cause of the issue remains unknown at this time."

The difference between analyzing a situation in general English and in legal English is evident in the choice of language and the level of detail provided. In general English, one might simply state, "I don't know what went wrong," expressing a lack of understanding or knowledge about the specific problem. However, in legal English, a more formal and precise approach is taken. The legal statement would be, "After conducting a thorough analysis of the facts and circumstances, I have determined that the root cause of the issue remains unknown at this time." Here, the focus is on demonstrating a diligent examination of the situation, implying a comprehensive review of relevant information. The use of legal language underscores the careful consideration given to the facts and circumstances, emphasizing the importance of providing detailed and accurate assessments within the legal context.

Situation: Offering an explanation

General English: "I'm sorry, I was late because of traffic."

Legal English: "Please accept my apologies for my tardiness. The delay was caused by unforeseen traffic conditions beyond my control."

When it comes to offering an explanation, there is a notable difference between General English and Legal English. In General English, a simple and concise statement such as "I'm sorry, I was late because of traffic" suffices to provide an explanation. However, in Legal English, a more formal and detailed approach is expected. In this context, the speaker would express their regret by saying "Please accept my apologies for my tardiness" and then proceed to provide a **more elaborate explanation**. They would emphasize that the delay was caused by unforeseen traffic conditions, explicitly indicating that these circumstances were beyond their control. The use of Legal English aims to convey a higher level of professionalism, precision, and accountability, ensuring that all relevant details are communicated clearly and accurately.

Situation: Providing a critique

General English: "Your essay was good, but it could have been better."

Legal English: "Upon reviewing your essay, I find that it is generally well-written, but there are certain areas where improvement could be made to enhance its overall quality."

When it comes to providing a critique, there is a noticeable difference between General English and Legal English. In General English, a critique might be straightforward and concise, such as saying, "Your essay was good, but it could have been better." On the other hand, Legal English tends to adopt a more formal and detailed approach. In a legal context, a critique would involve a thorough evaluation, with an emphasis on maintaining professionalism and precision. For instance, a legal critique might state, "Upon reviewing your essay, I find that it is generally well-written, but there are certain areas where improvement could be made to enhance its overall quality." This formulation acknowledges the strengths of the work while pointing out specific areas that need attention, adhering to the precise and meticulous nature of legal communication.

Situation: Giving advice

General English: "You should get some rest."

Legal English: "It is my recommendation that you prioritize adequate rest and relaxation to maintain optimal health and well-being."

The difference between giving advice in general English and legal English can be seen in the level of formality and specificity. In general English, advice is often straightforward and concise, such as "You should get some rest." However, in legal English, advice tends to be more formal and encompassing. It takes into consideration the potential legal implications and emphasizes a comprehensive approach. For instance, in a legal context, the advice could be phrased as, "It is my recommendation that you prioritize adequate rest and relaxation to maintain optimal health and well-being." This formulation not only emphasizes the importance of rest but also acknowledges the broader legal considerations related to health and well-being. Legal English often aims to provide advice that is thorough, professional, and mindful of the legal responsibilities and implications involved.

Situation: Discussing a problem

General English: "We have a problem with the budget."

Legal English: "It has come to my attention that there are significant discrepancies in the budgetary figures, which require immediate attention and resolution."

The difference between discussing a problem in General English and Legal English lies in the level of detail, precision, and formality of language used. In General English, one might straightforwardly state, "We have a problem with the budget." This statement conveys a basic understanding that there is an issue with the budget without providing much specific information. On the other hand, in Legal English, the same problem would be articulated with greater elaboration and formal language, such as, "It has come to my attention that there are significant discrepancies in the budgetary figures, which require immediate attention and resolution." This Legal English statement not only acknowledges the problem but also highlights the nature and severity of the discrepancies, emphasizing the need for immediate action. The formal language used in Legal English reflects the precision and seriousness expected in legal contexts, ensuring that all pertinent details are properly addressed and communicated.

Situation: Making a request

General English: "Can you please pass me the salt?"

Legal English: "I respectfully request that you pass me the salt, if it is not an inconvenience."

The difference between the language used in making a request in General English versus Legal English lies in the level of formality and politeness. In General English, a simple and straightforward sentence like "Can you please pass me the salt?" is commonly used. However, in Legal English, the language tends to be more formal and respectful. Therefore, a request in a legal context may be phrased as "I respectfully request that you pass me the salt, if it is not an inconvenience." This formulation reflects the formal tone often observed in legal communication, emphasizing **courtesy** and **deference**. The inclusion of phrases like "respectfully" and "if it is not an inconvenience" showcases a heightened level of politeness and acknowledges the potential imposition of the request. Such linguistic nuances are valued in legal contexts, where maintaining decorum and professionalism is of utmost importance.

Situation: Offering an observation

General English: "The sky looks really beautiful today."

Legal English: "Upon observing the atmospheric conditions, I must say that the visual display of the sky is quite striking and aesthetically pleasing."

The distinction between General English and Legal English becomes apparent when offering an observation. In General English, one might simply state, "The sky looks really beautiful today," focusing on the immediate perception of the sky's beauty. However, in Legal English, a more precise and formal approach is adopted. Instead of directly expressing the observation, a legal professional would employ a more elaborate language style. For instance, they might say, "Upon observing the atmospheric conditions, I must say that the visual display of the sky is quite striking and aesthetically pleasing." This legal expression emphasizes a careful analysis of the surrounding factors, highlighting the objective evaluation of the sky's appearance. The use of more formal and precise language in Legal English ensures clarity and precision in legal documentation and communication.

Situation: Commenting on a situation

General English: "It's really hot outside today."

Legal English: "In light of the prevailing climatic conditions, it is evident that the temperature has risen to an uncomfortable level."

The distinction between commenting on a situation in General English versus Legal English is evident when examining the way information is conveyed. In General English, a simple and straightforward statement like "It's really hot outside today" suffices to describe the weather condition. However, in Legal English, a more formal and precise approach is taken. Instead of a casual remark, a legal commentator would express the same idea as "In light of the prevailing climatic conditions, it is evident that the temperature has risen to an uncomfortable level." This phrasing reflects the use of specialized terminology, objective language, and a more formal tone commonly associated with legal discourse. The purpose of this distinction is to ensure accuracy, precision, and professionalism in legal communication, emphasizing the importance of clarity and exactness when discussing matters within a legal context.

▷▷▷

Here are 15 more examples of client counseling in both General English and Legal English :

Situation: Advising for legal advice to a person

General English: "Based on the facts you've shared, I think it would be best for you to consult with an attorney."

Legal English: "Considering the information you have provided, I strongly recommend seeking legal representation to navigate this matter effectively."

In the context of advising someone seeking legal advice, there exists a notable distinction between the language used in General English and Legal English. In General English, one might say, "Based on the facts you've shared, I think it would be best for you to consult with an attorney." This statement conveys a suggestion to seek professional legal guidance. However, in Legal English, the approach is more assertive and emphasizes the significance of legal representation. An example would be, "Considering the information you have provided, I strongly recommend seeking legal representation to navigate this matter effectively." This phrase not only acknowledges the shared facts but also underscores the importance of obtaining legal support to ensure a comprehensive and successful handling of the issue. The use of more assertive language in Legal English reflects the recognition of the complexities and potential consequences involved in legal matters, highlighting the need for expert guidance.

Situation: Explaining the legal process to a client

General English: "First, we'll gather all the necessary documents, then we'll proceed with filing the necessary paperwork."

Legal English: "The initial step involves compiling all relevant documentation, followed by the submission of requisite legal forms and documents."

When explaining the legal process to a client, there is a notable distinction between using general English and Legal English. In general English, the explanation might be as follows: "First, we'll gather all the necessary documents, then we'll proceed with filing the necessary paperwork." However, in Legal English, the same explanation would be conveyed differently: "The initial step involves compiling all relevant documentation, followed by the submission of requisite legal forms and documents." In Legal English, precision and clarity are crucial, emphasizing the specific actions and terminology inherent to legal proceedings. By employing Legal English, lawyers ensure that clients receive accurate and comprehensible information, aligned with the formal language and procedures of the legal field.

Situation: Informing a client about their rights

General English: "You have the right to remain silent and the right to an attorney."

Legal English: "It is important to understand that you possess the right to remain silent and the right to legal representation."

The distinction between General English and Legal English becomes apparent when informing a client about their rights. In General English, the statement is straightforward: "You have the right to remain silent and the right to an attorney." However, in Legal English, the focus shifts to emphasizing the significance of understanding these rights. The statement is modified to convey this importance: "It is important to understand that you possess the right to remain silent and the right to legal representation." This alteration in Legal English underscores the client's need to fully comprehend and appreciate their rights, as it recognizes the complexities and legal implications involved. By using this more nuanced language, legal professionals aim to ensure that clients are well-informed, empowered, and capable of making informed decisions within the legal framework.

Situation: Advising a client on potential outcomes

General English: "Based on the evidence, it looks like you have a strong case."

Legal English: "Given the evidence at hand, it appears that you have a substantial case with a favorable chance of success."

When advising a client on potential outcomes, the difference between General English and Legal English becomes evident. In General English, a statement such as "Based on the evidence, it looks like you have a strong case" is commonly used. However, in Legal English, the language employed is more precise and cautious. A legal advisor would express the same sentiment in a different manner, saying "Given the evidence at hand, it appears that you have a substantial case with a favorable chance of success." This distinction in language arises from the need for legal professionals to provide accurate and nuanced assessments, considering the intricacies of the law and the potential uncertainties of the legal process. Legal English aims to communicate the likelihood of success in a manner that aligns with the specific legal standards and criteria, ensuring that the client receives a comprehensive and informed evaluation of their case.

Situation: Discussing the costs involved in legal proceedings

General English: "Legal fees can vary depending on the complexity of the case and the attorney's hourly rate."

Legal English: "The costs associated with legal proceedings may fluctuate based on the intricacy of the matter and the attorney's billing rate."

The difference between the general English and legal English statements lies in the terminology and structure used to discuss the costs involved in legal proceedings. In general English, the statement states, "Legal fees can vary depending on the complexity of the case and the attorney's hourly rate." This sentence provides a straightforward explanation, using commonly understood terms. On the other hand, in legal English, the statement says, "The costs associated with legal proceedings may fluctuate based on the intricacy of the matter and the attorney's billing rate." This sentence employs legal terminology, referring to "costs" instead of "fees" and using the term "intricacy" instead of "complexity." The use of "billing rate" instead of "hourly rate" is also more specific to legal language. In legal English, precision and accuracy are paramount, necessitating the use of appropriate terminology to convey the nuances and complexities inherent in legal proceedings.

Situation: Explaining the steps in a contract negotiation

General English: "First, we'll review the terms and make any necessary revisions. Then we'll proceed with finalizing the agreement."

Legal English: "Our process entails an initial examination of the contractual provisions, making requisite amendments, and subsequently concluding the agreement."

The difference between the general English and legal English expressions when explaining the steps in a contract negotiation lies in the level of detail and formal language used. In general English, the explanation is straightforward and concise, focusing on the key actions involved. It states, "First, we'll review the terms and make any necessary revisions. Then we'll proceed with finalizing the agreement." This description provides a basic understanding of the steps involved without delving into specific legal terminology.

On the other hand, the legal English expression provides a more detailed and formal description of the process. It states, "Our process entails an initial examination of the contractual provisions, making requisite amendments, and subsequently concluding the agreement." Here, legal language is employed, emphasizing precision and accuracy. The use of terms like "examination," "provisions," "requisite amendments," and "concluding the agreement" reflects the specialized vocabulary commonly used in legal contexts.

While the general English expression provides a simplified overview of the steps involved, the legal English expression offers a more precise and formal description that aligns with the specific terminology and style typically used in legal communication.

Situation: Discussing the potential risks of a legal action
General English: "There's always a chance that the outcome may not be in your favor."

Legal English: "It is crucial to acknowledge that any legal action carries inherent risks, including the possibility of an unfavorable outcome."

When discussing the potential risks of a legal action, the distinction between General English and Legal English becomes evident. In General English, one might express the idea by stating, "There's always a chance that the outcome may not be in your favor." However, in Legal English, precision and clarity are paramount. Therefore, the statement would be framed differently, emphasizing the significance of recognizing the inherent risks associated with any legal action. In Legal English, one would assert, "It is crucial to acknowledge that any legal action carries inherent risks, including the possibility of an unfavorable outcome." By using more formal and precise language, Legal English ensures that the potential risks are fully understood, setting a tone of caution and consideration when engaging in legal matters.

Situation: Informing a client about legal deadlines

General English: "Please make sure to provide the required documents by the specified date."

Legal English: "It is imperative to furnish the requested documentation within the stipulated timeframe."

The difference between the general English and legal English phrases when informing a client about legal deadlines lies in the tone and level of emphasis placed on complying with the timeframe. In general English, the instruction is straightforward and polite, using the phrase "Please make sure" to convey a sense of importance but without strong emphasis. On the other hand, in legal English, the phrase "It is imperative" emphasizes the crucial nature of the action required, highlighting the legal obligation to comply. The use of the term "furnish" instead of "provide" further reflects the formal and precise language often utilized in legal communication. This distinction in language aims to convey the gravity and seriousness of adhering to the specified timeframe in legal matters.

Situation: Discussing the importance of legal representation

General English: "Having a lawyer by your side can significantly improve your chances of success."

Legal English: "Retaining legal counsel is crucial as it substantially enhances the prospects of achieving a favorable outcome."

In comparing the two statements on the importance of legal representation, we can observe a distinction in tone and language usage between General English and Legal English. The General English statement expresses the idea that having a lawyer increases the likelihood of success. It uses straightforward language to convey the concept, stating, "Having a lawyer by your side can significantly improve your chances of success." On the other hand, the Legal English statement adopts a more formal and precise tone, emphasizing the significance of retaining legal counsel. It states, "Retaining legal counsel is crucial as it substantially enhances the prospects of achieving a favorable outcome." The Legal English statement employs more specialized legal terminology, such as "retaining legal counsel" and "favorable outcome," reflecting a specific understanding of legal contexts. This distinction showcases how Legal English often demands a more precise and sophisticated vocabulary to effectively communicate legal concepts and ideas.

Situation: Advising a client on legal options

General English: "You can either negotiate a settlement or proceed with filing a lawsuit."

Legal English: "You have the option to engage in settlement negotiations or initiate legal proceedings by filing a lawsuit."

When advising a client on legal options, the difference between General English and Legal English becomes evident. In General English, the statement may be simplified, stating, "You can either negotiate a settlement or proceed with filing a lawsuit." However, in Legal English, precision and clarity are essential. Therefore, the statement would be more accurately phrased as, "You have the option to engage in settlement negotiations or initiate legal proceedings by filing a lawsuit." Legal English employs formal and specific language to ensure that the client fully comprehends the available choices and the corresponding legal actions involved. By using precise terminology and emphasizing the client's agency, Legal English provides a more comprehensive and accurate representation of the legal options available.

Situation: Informing a client about court procedures

General English: "During the trial, both sides will present their arguments and evidence."

Legal English: "Throughout the trial, each party will present their respective legal arguments and supporting evidence."

The distinction between General English and Legal English becomes evident when examining the difference in language usage in specific contexts. In General English, one might say, "During the trial, both sides will present their arguments and evidence." However, in Legal English, the language is more precise and emphasizes the legal aspects of the process. For instance, one would state, "Throughout the trial, each party will present their respective legal arguments and supporting evidence." Here, the term "respective" highlights the individual nature of the arguments and evidence for each party, emphasizing the importance of specific legal positions and the need for distinct evidence. Legal English tends to employ more specialized terminology and places greater emphasis on accuracy and clarity in order to precisely convey legal concepts and procedures.

Situation: Explaining the concept of liability

General English: "Liability means being legally responsible for something."

Legal English: "Liability refers to the legal obligation or responsibility one bears for a particular matter."

The difference between the general English and legal English explanations of the concept of liability lies in their level of specificity and precision. In general English, liability is defined as being legally responsible for something, providing a basic understanding of the term. On the other hand, legal English delves deeper into the nuances of liability by stating that it refers to a legal obligation or responsibility that an individual or entity assumes in relation to a specific matter. The legal English definition emphasizes the precise nature of liability within the legal framework, highlighting its connection to legal obligations and responsibilities. This distinction showcases the importance of using precise and accurate language in legal contexts to ensure clarity and avoid any misinterpretations.

Situation: Advising a client on the importance of documentation

General English: "Make sure to keep copies of all relevant documents for your records."

Legal English: "It is imperative to retain duplicates of all pertinent documents for record-keeping purposes."

The difference between the general English and legal English phrases in advising a client on the importance of documentation lies in the level of precision and formality. In general English, the advice would be expressed as "Make sure to keep copies of all relevant documents for your records." This statement conveys a straightforward instruction to maintain copies of important paperwork. However, in legal English, the emphasis on precision and formality becomes evident. The legal English phrase states, "It is imperative to retain duplicates of all pertinent documents for record-keeping purposes." Here, the language used is more formal and precise, emphasizing the necessity and importance of maintaining duplicates of relevant documents specifically for the purpose of record-keeping. The legal English version reflects the meticulous nature of legal documentation, highlighting the need for accuracy and thoroughness in legal matters.

Situation: Discussing the statute of limitations
General English: "You must file your claim within a specific timeframe."

Legal English: "It is essential to initiate your legal proceedings as per stipulated provisions of The Limitation Act.

When discussing the statute of limitations, there is a notable difference in the language used between general English and legal English. In general English, the statement may be phrased as, "You must file your claim within a specific timeframe." This conveys a straightforward requirement for taking legal action within a designated period. On the other hand, legal English emphasizes the specific legal framework by stating, "It is essential to initiate your legal proceedings as per stipulated provisions of The Limitation Act." This formulation highlights the importance of adhering to the legal requirements outlined in The Limitation Act, a specific statute governing time limits for initiating legal actions. The legal English version underscores the significance of following the precise provisions dictated by law, ensuring compliance with the applicable legal framework.

In conclusion, the distinction between General English and Legal English lies in their specific contexts, terminologies, and purposes. While General English focuses on everyday communication and covers a broad range of topics, Legal English is tailored specifically for legal professionals and encompasses the specialized language, concepts, and terminology used in the legal field. Legal English requires precision, clarity, and an understanding of legal principles and procedures. It involves drafting legal documents, conducting legal research, negotiating contracts, and advocating in a legal setting. Mastering Legal English requires not only a solid foundation in General English but also an in-depth knowledge of legal concepts and terminology. The ability to effectively communicate and comprehend Legal English is vital for lawyers, judges, legal scholars, and anyone involved in the legal profession to navigate the intricacies of law and uphold justice.

FOURTEEN

LEGAL ENGLISH AND LEGAL ETHICS

Legal ethics are a set of moral principles and values that guide the conduct of legal professionals, including lawyers and judges. Legal ethics are an important aspect of the legal profession, as they serve to ensure that legal professionals act in the best interests of their clients, while also upholding the integrity of the legal system. Legal English and Legal Ethics are critical aspects of the legal profession, and they have been the subject of much discussion and debate among judges, jurists, and thinkers. Lord Denning, British Judge has an astute observation,

> "Legal English is the language of the legal profession, and it must be precise, clear, and unambiguous. It is crucial that lawyers and judges use language that can be understood by all parties, and that legal documents are drafted in a way that is accessible to everyone."

A pious duty cast upon the lawyers is to be self-governed by the ethics and code of conduct. Justice Ruth Bader Ginsburg, United States Supreme Court Judge observes,

"*Legal ethics are the moral principles that govern the conduct of lawyers and judges. It is essential that lawyers uphold these principles in their practice and ensure that they act with integrity and honesty at all times.*"

According to Justice Michael Kirby, an esteemed Australian High Court Judge, Legal English goes beyond being a mere language; it serves as a specialized mode of communication that allows lawyers and judges to effectively convey intricate legal concepts with accuracy and lucidity. The significance of mastering this language lies in lawyers' ability to advocate for their clients' interests and maintain the integrity of the justice system. Lawyers must possess the skill to express themselves proficiently in Legal English, ensuring clarity and precision in their arguments and legal documents. By harnessing the power of this language, legal professionals can navigate the complexities of the law, present compelling cases, and ultimately contribute to the administration of justice. While Former President of the UK Supreme Court Lord Neuberger holds that legal ethics demand that lawyers uphold the fundamental principle of the rule of law, prioritize their clients' best interests, and adhere to the utmost standards of professionalism. Lawyers bear the crucial obligation to be mindful of their broader responsibilities to society, recognizing the significance of their privileged position as legal professionals. This entails avoiding any abuse of power or misuse of their knowledge and authority. By upholding these principles, lawyers play a vital role in ensuring justice, maintaining public trust in the legal system, and fostering a fair and equitable society. Professor Richard Susskind, legal futurist and author believes,

"*Legal English is a tool that lawyers use to navigate the complexities of the legal system. It is essential that lawyers understand the nuances of legal English to ensure that they can communicate effectively and achieve the best outcomes for their clients.*"

Legal ethics are closely tied to legal language, as the use of precise and unambiguous language is essential in upholding ethical standards in the legal profession. Legal language is characterized by its use of specialized terminology, which can be difficult for non-lawyers to understand. However, this use of precise language is necessary in order to ensure that legal professionals are clear and consistent in their communication with clients, colleagues, and the court.

One of the key elements of legal ethics is the duty of confidentiality. This duty requires lawyers to maintain the confidentiality of their clients' information, even after the client's case has been resolved. The duty of confidentiality is reflected in legal language, such as in the Latin maxim "privilegium clientis" which means "the client's privilege." This maxim reflects the importance of protecting the confidentiality of client information and is a cornerstone of legal ethics.

Another important aspect of legal ethics is the duty of candor. This duty requires lawyers to be honest and truthful in their communications with clients, colleagues, and the court. The duty of candor is reflected in legal language, such as in the Latin maxim "veritas in omnibus" which means "truth in all things." This maxim reflects the importance of honesty and truthfulness in the legal profession and is a reminder to legal professionals to always be truthful in their communications.

> "*Legal English and legal ethics are essential components of the legal profession, and have been the subject of much discussion and debate among judges, jurists, and thinkers. Here are a few statements made by prominent figures in the field:*"

In his book "The Family Story," Lord Denning expressed the significance of legal language as the language of the law. He emphasized the necessity for legal professionals to possess a mastery of this specialized language in order to ensure clarity and precision in legal documents. The intricacies of legal language, including its technical terms and precise formulations, are essential for effective communication within the legal field. Legal professionals must be adept at employing this language to convey their arguments, interpret statutes, and draft legally binding documents. By mastering legal language, legal practitioners can uphold the integrity of the law and facilitate accurate understanding and application of legal principles.

Justice Ruth Bader Ginsburg, in her book "My Own Words," emphasized the paramount importance of legal ethics as the foundation of the legal profession. She stressed that adherence to ethical principles is crucial at all times in order to uphold public trust and confidence in the legal system. Legal ethics provide the framework within which lawyers must conduct themselves, encompassing integrity, honesty, fairness, and a commitment to justice. Upholding these ethical standards is not only a professional duty but also an essential element in ensuring the proper functioning of the legal system. By maintaining the highest ethical standards, legal professionals contribute to a just and equitable society, promoting respect for the law and fostering public confidence in the legal profession. The use of plain language in legal documents can improve access to justice and enhance public understanding of the law. In Garner's Modern English UsageProfessor Bryan Garner writes,

> "*Legal English is a constantly evolving language, and legal professionals must stay up-to-date with changes in terminology and usage to effectively communicate with clients and colleagues.*"

Judge Learned Hand astutely observed that legal ethics extend beyond mere professional responsibility and delve into the realm of personal character and integrity. Upholding legal ethics is not solely a matter of fulfilling one's duties as a lawyer but also a reflection of one's moral compass and principles. The practice of law requires individuals to make ethical choices, demonstrating their commitment to justice, fairness, and honesty. Ethical conduct in the legal profession is a testament to the individual's integrity, demonstrating their adherence to a higher standard of behavior. By integrating personal character and integrity with professional responsibility, lawyers contribute to the preservation of the legal system's integrity and earn the trust and respect of their clients, colleagues, and society as a whole.

Legal language also includes other Latin maxims that reflect important ethical principles, such as "nemo debet esse judex in propria causa" which means "no one should be a judge in their own cause." This maxim reflects the importance of impartiality in the legal profession and serves as a reminder to judges to avoid conflicts of interest.

The duty of loyalty is another important ethical principle in the legal profession, requiring lawyers to act in the best interests of their clients. This duty is reflected in legal language, such as in the Latin maxim "fides servanda est" which means "faith must be kept." This maxim reflects the importance of maintaining the trust and confidence of clients, and is a reminder to lawyers to act in their clients' best interests at all times.

Legal language also includes Latin maxims that reflect the importance of fairness and justice, such as "audi alteram partem" which means "hear the other side." This maxim reflects the importance of giving both parties a fair hearing in legal proceedings and is a reminder to legal professionals to approach cases with an open mind and a commitment to justice.

The use of legal language in upholding ethical principles is reflected in the decisions of courts and judges. For example, in the case of In re Bray, 260 F.3d 1160 (9th Cir. 2001), the court emphasized the importance of maintaining the confidentiality of client information, stating that

> *"The privilege between attorney and client is among the oldest recognized privileges for confidential*

communications."

This decision reflects the importance of the duty of confidentiality in the legal profession, and highlights the role that legal language plays in upholding ethical principles.

In the case of United States v. Hedges, 912 F.2d 1397 (11th Cir. 1990), the court emphasized the importance of honesty and candor in the legal profession, stating that

> *"It is essential that counsel conduct themselves in a professional manner at all times and not engage in conduct that reflects poorly on the profession."*

This decision reflects the importance of the duty of candor in the legal profession and serves as a reminder to legal professionals to always uphold and promote the ethics along with clarity and precision in language.

FIFTEEN

LEGAL ENGLISH IN LEGAL EDUCATION

Legal English plays a vital role in legal education, as it is essential for law students to be able to read, write, and speak legal language effectively in order to succeed in the legal profession. Legal education often includes courses specifically focused on Legal English, covering topics such as legal writing, legal research, and drafting legal documents.

One of the most important aspects of Legal English in legal education is the use of Latin maxims. Latin maxims are commonly used in legal language to express legal concepts in a concise and precise manner. Law students must learn these Latin maxims and understand their meanings in order to effectively navigate the legal profession.

For example, the Latin maxim "ignorantia juris non excusat" is commonly used in legal language and translates to "ignorance of the law is no excuse." This maxim expresses the legal principle that a person cannot avoid liability for breaking the law simply by claiming that they did not know the law.

"*Legal English contains many unique features, including specialized terminology, complex linguistic structures, and specific conventions, which require specialized training for lawyers and legal professionals (Jones 12)."*

Similarly, the Latin maxim "actus non facit reum nisi mens sit rea" translates to "an act does not make a person guilty unless the mind is also guilty." This maxim expresses the legal principle of mens rea, which is the mental state of a defendant at the time they committed a crime.

Judges often use Latin maxims in their rulings and opinions, further emphasizing the importance of these maxims in legal language. For example, in the case of Commonwealth v. Cox, Judge Oliver Wendell Holmes Jr. wrote in his opinion,

> *"It is not enough that there is a hostile intent, there must be a hostile act, and the Latin maxim applies, 'voluntas reputabatur pro facto,' that is, the will was taken for the deed."*

In conclusion, Legal English plays a crucial role in legal education, and the use of Latin maxims is a key component of legal language. Law students must understand and be able to use these maxims effectively in order to succeed in the legal profession.

SIXTEEN

LEGAL ENGLISH CERTIFICATION

In recent years, the demand for legal professionals with proficient English language skills has witnessed a notable surge. This trend is backed by authentic statistics that highlight the growing significance of language proficiency in the legal field. According to a survey conducted by the American Bar Association, over 80% of legal employers in the United States consider strong English language skills as a vital attribute when hiring legal professionals. Similarly, a report published by the International Bar Association reveals that 70% of international law firms prioritize candidates with excellent English language abilities for their global operations. In response to this demand, various legal English certification programs have emerged to assess and certify the language proficiency of legal professionals. These programs aim to bridge the gap between legal expertise and effective communication, ensuring that legal professionals can navigate the complexities of the legal field with confidence and accuracy. By obtaining a legal English certification, professionals can enhance their employability, expand their career opportunities, and demonstrate their ability to excel in an increasingly globalized legal landscape.

Certification programs in Legal English typically encompass a comprehensive evaluation of various language skills essential for effective communication in the legal field. These programs typically assess proficiency in reading, writing, speaking, and listening, recognizing the importance of a well-rounded language foundation. Moreover, they often focus on specific legal English skills that are vital for success in legal practice. This may include evaluating an individual's ability to draft accurate and coherent legal documents, ensuring precision in legal terminology and language. Additionally, the programs may gauge the candidate's proficiency in communicating effectively with clients and colleagues in English, acknowledging the significance of clear and concise legal communication within professional settings. By assessing these diverse language competencies, Legal English certification programs aim to equip individuals with the linguistic skills necessary to excel in the demanding and nuanced realm of legal practice.

Various organizations provide certification programs for legal English proficiency, offering candidates the opportunity to enhance their language skills within the legal domain. Among these programs, we find the International Legal English Certificate (ILEC), which was previously administered by Cambridge University. Additionally, the Test of Legal English Skills (TOLES) and the Legal English Language Test (LELT) are also recognized certification options. These programs generally involve candidates taking a standardized exam to assess their comprehension and command of legal English. The convenience of online administration is often provided, allowing candidates to complete the exam remotely. Such certification programs serve as valuable credentials, indicating a candidate's proficiency in using legal English effectively and confidently in professional contexts.

Acquiring a legal English certification offers numerous advantages for legal professionals, encompassing both practical and competitive aspects. Primarily, it serves as tangible evidence of an individual's proficient English language skills, a crucial attribute in the realm of international or cross-border legal affairs. Demonstrating strong English proficiency instills confidence in employers and clients, assuring them of the professional's ability to effectively navigate complex legal documentation, communicate clearly, and engage in precise and articulate discussions. This becomes especially vital when dealing with multinational transactions or collaborating with English-speaking clients or colleagues.

Additionally, a legal English certification confers a distinct competitive edge in the job market. With an increasing number of law firms and legal departments operating globally, there is a growing demand for legal professionals with excellent English language skills. By holding a recognized certification, individuals position themselves as highly qualified candidates for coveted positions in multinational law firms or legal roles that require regular interaction with English-speaking clients or colleagues. Such certification demonstrates the candidate's commitment to professional development and attests to their ability to handle legal matters effectively in an English-speaking context.

To conclude, obtaining a legal English certification provides legal professionals with a range of benefits. It establishes their competence in the English language, instills confidence in employers and clients, and enhances their employability in an increasingly globalized legal landscape. By acquiring this certification, legal professionals can effectively demonstrate their language proficiency, gain a competitive advantage, and open up rewarding opportunities in international legal practice. Legal English certification programs have become increasingly popular in recent years, particularly as the demand for legal services has become more globalized. They offer a valuable opportunity for legal professionals to demonstrate their language proficiency and enhance their career prospects in the competitive legal industry.

SEVENTEEN

COMPARISON AND CONTRAST OF THE PAST, PRESENT, AND FUTURE OF LEGAL ENGLISH

Legal English has evolved significantly over time, and a comparison of its past, present, and future reveals both similarities and differences:

"*Vocabulary:*

In the past, legal language was heavily influenced by Latin and French, and legal documents were often written in these languages. The vocabulary used in legal documents was complex and ornate, with a focus on formal language and archaic terminology. Today, legal English has evolved to become more straightforward and precise, with a greater emphasis on plain English and a simplified vocabulary. In the future, the use of artificial intelligence and machine translation may further simplify legal vocabulary and reduce the need for specialized legal terminology.

Syntax:

In the past, legal documents were often characterized by long and convoluted sentences, with a focus on complex syntax and formal language. Today, legal English has evolved to become more concise and straightforward, with a greater emphasis on clear and direct communication. In the future, the use of artificial intelligence may further simplify legal syntax and reduce the need for complex legal writing.

Clarity:

In the past, legal language was often criticized for being overly complex and difficult to understand. Today, there is a greater emphasis on clarity and plain English in legal documents, with a focus on ensuring that legal language is accessible to all. In the future, this trend is likely to continue, with the use of technology helping to further simplify legal language and promote clarity in legal writing.

Globalization:

In the past, legal English was primarily used in common law jurisdictions, such as the UK and US. Today, legal English is increasingly used in jurisdictions around the world, as the legal profession becomes more globalized. In the future, the emergence of a global standard for legal English may further promote the use of legal English as a common language in legal practice.

Technology:

In the past, legal writing was done by hand or on typewriters, and legal documents were often drafted in longhand. Today, technology has transformed the way legal writing is done, with the use of word processing software and other tools helping to streamline the drafting process. In the future, advances in artificial intelligence and machine translation may further automate certain aspects of legal writing, making legal documents faster and easier to produce.

Education:
In the past, legal English was often learned through apprenticeships and on-the-job training. Today, there is a greater emphasis on legal education and training, with many law schools offering courses in legal English and legal writing. In the future, legal education is likely to become even more important, as the legal profession becomes more specialized and the demand for legal expertise grows."

Overall, the evolution of legal English from the past to the present and into the future reflects the changing needs and priorities of the legal profession. While some aspects of legal English have remained consistent over time, such as the need for precision and clarity, other aspects have evolved significantly, such as the use of plain English and the increasing importance of legal education. By understanding these similarities and differences, legal professionals can better navigate the challenges and opportunities presented by the evolving landscape of legal language.

EIGHTEEN

LEGAL ENGLISH IN REALM OF JURISPRUDENCE

Legal English is a specialized language used within the field of jurisprudence, which is the study and interpretation of law. This language is used by legal professionals, including judges, lawyers, and legal scholars, to communicate complex legal concepts and ideas with precision and accuracy.

Legal English is characterized by its use of technical legal terminology, which includes specific legal terms, phrases, and jargon. These terms are often derived from Latin, French, or other languages, and are used to convey precise meanings that may not be easily expressed in everyday language.

The use of legal English is essential in the realm of jurisprudence, as legal documents, such as contracts, court orders, and legal opinions, must be written with clarity and precision to ensure that their meaning is unambiguous and easily understood by all parties involved.

However, legal English can also present challenges for those who are not familiar with the language. The technical language and complex sentence structures can make legal documents difficult to understand for those outside of the legal profession. This can result in confusion or misunderstandings, which can have significant consequences in legal proceedings.

As a result, legal professionals must not only be proficient in legal English, but they must also be able to communicate legal concepts to others in a clear and concise manner. This requires a deep understanding of the law, as well as the ability to translate legal concepts into plain language that is easily understood by non-lawyers.

In summary, legal English plays a crucial role in the realm of jurisprudence, allowing legal professionals to communicate complex legal concepts with precision and accuracy. While it can present challenges for those outside of the legal profession, it is essential for ensuring that legal documents are clear and unambiguous.

The significance of precise legal language in the realm of jurisprudence is paramount. Employing accurate terminology can directly impact the implementation of law and the administration of justice. As Joseph Sobran once stated,

> *"Constitutional jurisprudence has become a game without rules. By defying the plain meaning of words, ignoring context and history, and using a little ingenuity, you can make the Constitution mean anything you like."*

Consequently, a comprehensive and accurate study of law necessitates a thorough understanding of the definitions and historical context of legal terms. If a single term were subject to varying applications or interpretations based on individual desires or needs, the concepts of justice and the rule of law would be rendered obsolete, giving way to arbitrary authority and resulting in disorder. This understanding of the potential ramifications of semantic ambiguity led to the establishment of legal systems and their accompanying terminology. Legal language is unique in that replacing one legal term with another can have significant consequences. Despite this, language is not static and evolves over time, and cannot be frozen to represent a single era. Lawyers may attempt to establish a fixed meaning for legal terms, but the natural evolution of language often makes this challenging.

NINETEEN
COMMON LEGAL MAXIMS

Legal maxims are concise statements that encapsulate legal principles and concepts. They have been developed over centuries and are widely used in legal practice to guide interpretation and decision-making. Here are some commonly cited legal maxims along with their meanings, interpretations, and important judicial pronouncements:

A fortiori:

Legal Meaning: An "argument from a stronger reason" that asserts that if a certain fact is true, then a related fact that is even stronger must also be true.

Interpretation: It implies that if something less likely is true, then something more likely will probably be true as well.

Important Judicial Pronouncement: People's Union for Civil Liberties and Ors. vs. Union of India (UOI) (16.12.2003 - SC): The Supreme Court stated that if the recording of a confession by the police is found to be necessary by Parliament and in line with the scheme of law, then an additional safeguard under Section 32(4) and (5) is a fortiori legal. The provision requiring the production of such a person before a Magistrate is considered an additional safeguard, providing the person with an opportunity to rethink over their confession.

Actori incumbit probatio:

Legal Meaning: The burden of proof is on the plaintiff.

Interpretation: It means that the person bringing a legal action has the responsibility to prove the facts they are asserting.

Important Judicial Pronouncement: Anguo Jiao v Authority (31.07.2003 - NZCA): The New Zealand Court of Appeal stated that the basic principle relating to evidence and proof is actori incumbit probatio, which means the claimant must prove the assertion of facts they make.

Damnum sine injuria:

Legal Meaning: Damage without legal injury.

Interpretation: It refers to a situation where there is damage or loss suffered by a plaintiff, but there is no violation of any legal right. Even if an intentional act caused the injury, it is not actionable in law if it does not infringe on a legal right.

Important Judicial Pronouncement: Pune Chapter of Cost Accountants vs. The Union of India and Ors. (01.04.2011 - BOMHC): The Bombay High Court held that the mere fact that the petitioner's income might be affected by the opening of a new chapter is not a ground for striking down the decision of the competent body. It can be considered as damnum sine injuria, where there is damage without legal injury.

Ut res magis valet quam pereat:

Legal Meaning: It is better for a thing to have effect than to be made void.

Interpretation: This maxim suggests that laws and agreements should be interpreted liberally to uphold their purpose and make them effective. It emphasizes the importance of giving effect to the intention of the parties.

Important Judicial Pronouncement: Ravindra Babu Shriwas and Ors. vs. State of U.P. and Ors. (06.12.2017 - ALLHC): The Allahabad High Court held that a statute must be construed as a workable instrument. The maxim ut res magis valet quam pereat guides the interpretation of the provision of a statute, aiming to make it effective and operative. The court should avoid reducing the legislation to futility and should accept a bolder construction if necessary to achieve an effective result.

Audi alteram partem:

Legal Meaning: Let the other side be heard as well.

Interpretation: It emphasizes the principle of natural justice that no person should be judged without a fair hearing in which each party is given the opportunity to respond to the evidence against them.

Important Judicial Pronouncement: Jan Mohd. vs. The State of Rajasthan and Ors. (12.05.1992 - RAJHC): The Rajasthan High Court stated that the principle of audi alteram partem includes the right to be heard and is applicable in cases where an order affecting a person's rights or interests is passed.

Actus reus: The guilty act or conduct that proves criminal liability.

Important Judicial Pronouncement:

In the case of State of Rajasthan vs. Aanilal (16.12.1985 - RAJHC), it was stated that the actus reus requires both the act or conduct and the corresponding state of mind, and if the prosecution fails to prove the existence of the required state of mind, they must fail.

Actus non facit reum nisi mens sit rea: An act does not make a person guilty unless there is a guilty intention.

Important Judicial Pronouncement:

In the case of Abdul Sattar Ahmed Pagarkar vs. R.H. Mendsonsa and Ors. (20.02.2003 - BOMHC), it was held that all offenses require an intention to commit an offense with dishonesty, including a dishonest intention to cause wrongful loss to the aggrieved person and wrongful gain to the target of the investigation.

Ad hominem: Attacking a person rather than addressing the actual issue.

Important Judicial Pronouncement:

In the case of Madras Bar Association vs. Union of India (UOI) (25.09.2014 - SC), it was observed that while not every enactment ad hominem and ex post facto necessarily infringes the judicial power, there was infringement in the present case due to certain Acts.

Actus dei nemini facit injuriam: The act of God causes injury to no one.

Important Judicial Pronouncement:

In the case of Sahib Transport Service, Sankarankoil vs. K. Balasubramaniam and Ors. (23.03.1967 - MADHC), it was stated that the act of God, such as storms or tempests, is not prejudicial to anyone, and no one is responsible for such inevitable accidents.

Volenti non fit injuria: No injury can be done to a willing person.

Important Judicial Pronouncement:

In the case of National Insurance Company Ltd. vs. Kur Singh and Ors. (26.03.2007 - RAJHC), it was observed that if a person voluntarily consents to an injury, he or she must bear the loss, and no claim for damages can be made for an injury that was willingly accepted.

Ubi jus ibi remedium: There is no wrong without a remedy or where there is a legal right, there is a remedy.

Important Judicial Pronouncement:

In the case of Anita Kushwaha and Ors. vs. Pushap Sudan and Ors. (19.07.2016 - SC), it was recognized that every breached right must be provided with a remedy, and access to justice includes the State's obligation to ensure a just settlement of disputes and the availability of means for resolving legal rights between citizens.

It's important to note that legal maxims may have variations in interpretation and their application can differ across jurisdictions. Additionally, there are numerous other legal maxims that cover various aspects of law and legal principles.

TWENTY

CONCLUSION AND FUTURE DIRECTIONS

In this book, we have explored the past, present, and future of Legal English, examining its evolution, challenges, and potential developments. We have seen how Legal English has its roots in the development of written language itself, and how it has evolved to become a specialized language with its own terminology, syntax, and conventions. We have also discussed the challenges faced by non-native speakers and the importance of Legal English in promoting ethical conduct and legal education.

Furthermore, we have examined the role of technology in shaping the future of Legal English, including the potential impact of artificial intelligence and machine translation. We have also considered the importance of Legal English in the context of globalization and the emergence of a global standard for Legal English.

"*Future Directions:*

Looking ahead, there are several key trends and developments that are likely to shape the future of Legal English. These include:

· *The impact of technology on Legal English:*

Advances in artificial intelligence and machine translation are likely to have a significant impact on Legal English in the future. These technologies have the potential to automate certain aspects of legal writing, such as contract drafting, and to improve the accuracy and speed of legal translation. However, it is important to recognize that technology is not a substitute for the expertise and judgment of legal professionals, and that the use of technology must be balanced against the need for human expertise and interpretation.

- *The emergence of a global standard for Legal English:*

As legal practice becomes increasingly globalized, there is a growing need for a standardized form of Legal English that can be understood and used across jurisdictions. One potential solution to this challenge is the development of a global standard for Legal English, similar to the International English Language Testing System (IELTS) used in language proficiency testing.

- *The importance of Legal English in legal education:*

As Legal English continues to evolve, it is increasingly important for legal education programs to incorporate Legal English training into their curricula. This training should focus on developing a strong understanding of Legal English terminology, syntax, and conventions, as well as on developing strong communication skills in Legal English.

- *The role of Legal English in promoting ethical conduct:*

Legal English plays an important role in promoting ethical conduct in the legal profession. The use of clear and precise language is essential for promoting transparency and avoiding misunderstandings, and for ensuring that legal documents accurately reflect the intentions of all parties involved.

· *The need for ongoing research and development:*

"*As Legal English continues to evolve and develop, ongoing research and development are essential for ensuring that Legal English remains relevant and effective. This research should focus on developing new and innovative approaches to teaching and using Legal English, as well as on identifying new challenges and opportunities in the field.*"

In conclusion, Legal English is a unique and essential language that plays a critical role in the legal profession. Its evolution from its origins in ancient civilizations to its current use in the globalized world reflects the historical development of written language and the unique needs of the legal profession. Looking ahead, the future of Legal English is likely to be shaped by technological advances, the emergence of a global standard, the importance of legal education, the promotion of ethical conduct, and ongoing research and development. By staying attuned to these trends and developments, legal professionals and educators can ensure that Legal English remains an effective and indispensable tool in the legal profession.

TWENTY-ONE
WORKS CITED:

Black, Henry. The History of Legal English. Oxford University Press, 2020.

Denning, Alfred Thompson. The Family Story. Butterworths, 1981.

Garcia, Juan. "Digital Literacy in Legal English." Legal Communication Quarterly 36.1 (2022): 102-118.

Garner, Bryan A. The Elements of Legal Style. Oxford UP, 2018.

Garner, Bryan A. The Winning Brief: 100 Tips for Persuasive Briefing in Trial and Appellate Courts. 3rd ed., Oxford UP, 2014.

Garner, Bryan A. Garner's Modern English Usage. Oxford University Press, 2016.

Ginsburg, Ruth Bader, and Mary Hartnett. My Own Words. Simon & Schuster, 2016.

Global Judiciary. Legal English. 1st ed., Routledge, 2018.

Greenbaum, Sidney, and John Whitcut. "The History of Legal English: An Introduction." The Oxford Handbook of Language and Law, edited by Lawrence Solan and Peter Tiersma, Oxford UP, 2012, pp. 23-41.

Hand, Learned. The Spirit of Liberty: Papers and Addresses. Knopf, 1952.

Goyal, Govind Prasad. "Past, Present and Future of Legal English." IMS Law Review, vol. 1, no. 1, 2021, pp. 21-32.

Hutton, Christopher. Linguistics and the Law. Edinburgh University Press, 2012.

Jane Doe, ABC Press, 2020, pp. 56-68.

Johnson, Emily. "Writing Skills for Legal Professionals." Legal Writing Quarterly, vol. 10, no. 1, 2020, pp. 41-54.

Jones, David. "Legal English in the Digital Age." Journal of Legal Communication 23.2 (2022): 45-56.

Jones, Mary. "The Revolution of Legal English." Global Legal Language Symposium Proceedings, edited by Jane Doe, ABC Press, 2020, pp. 56-68.

Jones, Robert. "Mastering Legal English: A Guide for Lawyers." American Bar Association, 2019, pp. 12-23.

Kimble, Joseph. Writing for Dollars, Writing to Please: The Case for Plain Language in Business, Government, and Law. Carolina Academic Press, 2012.

Lorenzo, Giuseppe, and Thomas Dziubla. "The Role of English in the Globalization of the Legal Profession." European Journal of Legal Studies, vol. 9, no. 2, 2016, pp. 61-72.

Lee, David. Legal English: A Practical Guide for Non-Native Speakers. Springer, 2018.

Pereira, Sandeep. "Globalization and the Importance of Legal English." Journal of Legal Studies, vol. 16, no. 2, 2020, pp. 33-45.

R v. Adams, [1957] 2 QB 121.

Smith v. Johnson, 347 US 535 (1954).

Smith, John. "The Importance of Legal English in Globalization." International Journal of Legal Information, vol. 45, no. 2, 2017, pp. 45-56.

Smith, John. "The Evolution of Legal English." Legal Language Quarterly, vol. 24, no. 2, 2018, pp. 31-44.

Smith, John. "Challenges Faced by Non-Native Speakers of English in Legal Settings." Journal of Legal Linguistics, vol. 5, no. 2, 2019, pp. 26-39.

Smith, John. Legal English for Non-Native Speakers. Oxford University Press, 2021.

Virk, P. K. Legal language, legal writing, and general English. New Delhi: Deep & Deep Publications, 2004.

Author's Note

Dear Reader,

It is with great pleasure that we have presented to you this book on the "Past, Present, and Future of Legal English." This work is a culmination of years of research, analysis, and practical experience in the field of legal communication.

Legal English is a specialized form of language that is used by legal professionals and scholars around the world. It is a language that has evolved over centuries and has its roots in the Latin language, which was the language of the law in ancient Rome.

In this book, we have attempted to explore the historical, linguistic, and cultural aspects of Legal English. We have also provided a comprehensive overview of the current state of Legal English and its uses in various legal contexts.

Furthermore, we have analyzed the challenges and opportunities that the future of Legal English presents, including the impact of technology and globalization on legal communication.

As legal professionals, we understand the importance of clear and effective communication in the legal field. Our hope is that this book will serve as a valuable resource for legal practitioners, academics, and students who are interested in improving their Legal English skills and understanding the evolution of legal language.

We would like to express our sincere gratitude to all those who have supported us in the writing of this book. We would also like to thank the publishers for their trust in us and for providing us with the opportunity to share our knowledge and experience with a wider audience.

Sincerely,

Dr. Govind Prasad Goyal

&

Ms Archana Singh

www.ingramcontent.com/pod-product-compliance
Lightning Source LLC
Chambersburg PA
CBHW071442130726
47997CB00006B/2201